D0722469

THE
STORM
OF
SEX ADDICTION

RESCUE AND RECOVERY

CONNIE A. LOFGREEN
MSW, CSAT

STARPRO®
SEXUAL TREATMENT AND
RECOVERY PROGRAM
Omaha, Nebraska

FIRST EDITION

Cover design by Samuel Nudds
Layout design by Lorraine Box
ISBN 978-0-9857618-0-6
Library of Congress Control Number: 2012911879
Printed in the United States of America
www.connielofgreen.com

I knew a place onest and there was a time

Onest where there was nothing but good.

Ever been such a place?

Well, if'n you ever was then you'll know this funny kinda thing

I'm telling you.

Your heart starts hurtin' mighty early then, because of what you see.

Seems like you can see clearer, if'n you ever was in the good place.

And sometimes the only way to hold back hurtin'

Is to put that seeing part away.

Its like sending a good little 'ole kid far away, and it a greeving over that.

But you gotta do it, lessen your heart might just bust.

But then they'll come a time, later on,

When you got to bring that little kid back

And then you find out a funny thing.

Now you gotta go where the kid says and you're gonna be scared then

Because that little good kid you hid away is braver

And stronger and sees clearer than you do

And now you can't do nothing but go where the kid says

'Cause you owe a debt-like for hiding your eyes all those years

And sending that fresh eyed kid away.

—Liz Hofmeister

TABLE OF CONTENTS

PART ONE

THE STORM

CHAPTER ONE

THE STORM OF SEX ADDICTION

An Epidemic

What is happening under our eyes within the mass of peoples?
What is the cause of this disorder in society, this uneasy agitation,
these swelling waves, these whirling and mingling currents
and these turbulent and formidable new impulses?[1]

Teilhard de Chardin

The storm of sex addiction is brewing. It is a gathering danger, a looming national epidemic making landfall and breaching our societal levees. The threat is imminent for every family and the casualty count is rising. We are *all* in the path of the storm.

Sex addiction is a brain disorder characterized by the compulsive use of sexual behavior over which an addict has lost control. Sex addicts are attempting to escape reality by *mood-altering* using sex. As the illness progresses it wreaks havoc, creating chaos and misery in the lives of addicts and their families.

Sex addiction affects males and females of all ages (including children). The Society for the Advancement of Sexual Health suggests that approximately 3-5% of the population seek treatment, though

3

more could be afflicted; and statistical surveys suggest that 80% of sex addicts are male.[2] Online sexual activity, the "crack cocaine of sex addiction," is a major contributing factor and has spurred a multi-billion dollar Internet pornography (iPorn) industry.[3] As you may know, the majority of online searches are related to sex and pornography.

Using sex like a recreational drug may appear to be harmless and it is certainly in vogue; but such widespread re-direction of biological drives for sex, romance, and relationship, into excesses of sexual fantasy and behavior is unprecedented. The result is a growing storm of sex addiction that could create a social catastrophe of immense proportions. However, if forecast and confronted with a coordinated response, the storm may also present a remarkable opportunity for us as individuals, families, and society, to positively transform our personal lives and the ways in which we relate to one another. If we are to be a sexually responsible and sober society, we must do more than remediate the casualties—we must prevent the devastation.

Dark Clouds on the Horizon

The most stunning downfall of a public figure because of sexual transgressions may well be that of all-American golf hero Tiger Woods. As 2009 drew to a close, the glow of holiday celebrations was dimmed by news of a darker kind of merry-making. Emblazoned on TV screens and exploding from the headlines was the shocking story of the man many consider the most talented athlete of all time. In fewer strokes than it used to take him to sink a winning putt, Tiger Woods had jeopardized his career and his family, and betrayed the nation's adulation of him. With reports of his adulterous adventures rocking the world—in the course of a week some ten women came forth to tell all—Woods's product-endorsement income was predicted to be decimated by more than $150 million. As his wife fled their home, taking their young children with her, Tiger Woods's fate as a global golf champion and a squeaky-clean role model for young athletes everywhere hung in the balance.

Why would a man at the peak of his powers put everything he had worked so tirelessly to attain at risk for a blond brigade of "alleged mistresses"? What in Tiger Woods's life—now or in his past—drove him to this terrible moment?

Buzz Bissinger writes in *Vanity Fair*, "[I]t is safe to say that behind the non-accessible accessibility and seemingly perfect marriage to a beautiful woman was a sex addict who could not get enough."[4] Addiction expert Drew Pinsky, who hosted the TV program "*Sex Rehab with Dr. Drew*," also speculated Woods may be addicted to sex. Pinsky stated: "It's safe to say that sex addiction might be a part of his problem."[5] Indeed, Woods's compulsivity, loss of control, and the fact that he continued his risky behavior in spite of severe consequences— all hallmarks of sex addiction—suggested that this might be so. Of course, no one can make this claim without evaluating Woods in person. Interestingly, though, Pinsky noted that we may learn more about the cause and cure of this affliction as we observe how Woods seeks treatment and rebuilds his reputation. He did in fact apologize publicly and entered a treatment program for sex addiction.

The story of Tiger Woods is a sad one. He lost his marriage, disrupted the high-achievement of his career, imperiled his reputation, and had a "fan" throw a hot dog at him as a result of his infidelities. This would seem to indicate an uphill road, with long-term therapy in his future. It remains to be seen how he will piece his life back together, but he must have felt that firing his caddy was a good start. And after years of struggle, he finally achieved another PGA Tour victory.

In addition to Tiger Woods, the public has been reeling from media revelations of sex scandals that destroy the lives of both the glamorous and the ordinary. Politicians such as Anthony Weiner, who resigned after using social media to send underwear glamour shots; Senator and presidential candidate, John Edwards (love child and "legally" concealed mistress); Governor Eliot Spitzer (client "Number Nine"); Governor Mark Sanford (Argentinean "soul mate"); and Senator Larry Craig (airport bathroom stall "foot-tapper") are likely forever branded by their indiscretions.

TV star David Duchovny migrated from the "*X-Files*" to the triple-X files, to play a sex addicted writer on Showtime's "*Californication.*" Ironically, he later admitted himself to treatment for sex addiction. Debra LaFavre and Mary Kay Letourneau are the most infamous predecessors of a rapidly expanding list of classroom teacher sex offenders. Superstars of evangelism and priesthood have shamed themselves and their multi-million dollar ministries with their sexual misconduct. ESPN analyst Steve Phillips entered rehab for sex addiction after being fired from his job. Even David Letterman got in trouble, after an extortion scandal forced him to admit a series of affairs with young women on his staff. And Charlie Sheen may or may not really have been "winning" with his tireless pursuit of prostitutes and "goddesses."

We are often astonished and mystified by such reckless and seemingly irrational behavior, but we cannot diagnose Tiger Woods, Charlie Sheen, Penn State's Jerry Sandusky, or any other public figure. But what of people whom we can definitively identify as sex addicts, men and women who are deeply disturbed by their behavior and desperate to find the proper treatment? What do we know about how they got caught in the maelstrom of addiction and how they continue to subjugate their lives to this dangerous obsession?

In my thirty-plus years of private practice as a psychotherapist, I have evaluated and treated hundreds of men and women of all ages and racial and ethnic backgrounds—people whose out-of-control sexual behavior has caused them untold suffering—people who are determined to rid themselves of their compulsive activities. In the safety of my therapy office, they have shared their most shameful secrets, drilled down to their childhood memories, and bravely examined their self-destructive habits. They have helped me gain a fresh understanding of how sex addictions arise, how this disorder maintains a grip on its victims, and how, with help, sufferers can learn healthier and happier ways of living.

The Storm of Sex Addiction: Rescue and Recovery is intended to elevate the conversation about sex addiction. It is a clarion call for us as a society to address this illness. I have become increasingly concerned about the rising number of clients who struggle with sex addiction. You may be concerned because you or someone you know is struggling, too. This book is based on my years of experience as a marriage and family therapist and as a Certified Sex Addiction Therapist. It incorporates knowledge from my extensive work with adult survivors of childhood sexual abuse. *The Storm of Sex Addiction* explains the dynamics and roots of the disorder. It provides practical information and compassionate guidance to *anyone* affected by sex addition, especially the addicts and families whose lives it shatters. It will describe the hopeful process of recovery.

However, *The Storm* does more than sound the alarm and encourage treatment. It goes beyond the voyeuristic entertainment value of personal sex tragedies sensationalized in the media, and addresses the epidemic as the public health issue it truly is. *The Storm* envisions a new era of valuing authentic intimate relationships over reckless sexual consumption and exploitation.

Using Sex like a Drug

Although it is the last major addiction to be identified and researched, many clinicians believe sex addiction is not only a "real" addiction, but the ultimate addiction. As Sigmund Freud suggested, all others "may just be a substitute."[6] Modern neuroscience, via brain imaging, reveals that *all* addictions, including sex addiction, stimulate the same pleasure centers of the brain.

Sex addiction is to be included in the next edition of the *Diagnostic and Statistical Manual of Mental Disorders* (DSM-V) as a category called *hypersexual disorder*.[7] It is not yet to be included as "sex addiction" because studies are ongoing about its withdrawal effects, which seem to be similar to withdrawal from smoking—irritability, restlessness, insomnia, fatigue, and cravings.

Sex addiction falls within a spectrum of severe intimacy disorders, which include relationship addictions—codependency, romance addiction, love addiction/love avoidance, and trauma bonding. Sex and relationship addictions are characterized by dependence on sexual or emotional intensity as the "drug" of choice. Sex addicts stimulate sexual arousal and emotional intensity to become euphoric or "numb-out," much like substance addicts use cocaine or alcohol. Excessive use of mood-altering behaviors, rather than mood-altering substances, are a sex addict's path of escape from life stress and overwhelming emotions of loneliness, anger, fear, and shame.

Sex and relationship addictions are considered severe intimacy disorders because one's "significant other" is a mood-altering behavior rather than a real person. An addict lacks the skills to develop a close intimate relationship with a person, usually because these skills were not learned in early life. The intimacy disorder increases an addict's emotional isolation and loneliness, triggering further cycles of acting-out with sex to escape unbearable emotions.

Sex addiction often progresses to the point that an addict is risking everything for the euphoria and escapism of a sex "fix." Many addicts feel deep shame about acting outside their values, and fear the risks and consequences but are unable to quit. Others have ready excuses to minimize their problem or deny their addiction: "Everybody does it," "I just have an uninhibited lifestyle," or, "It's just sex."

How Is Sex Addiction Different?

We tend to envy starry-eyed lovers and idealize romantic love stories. Sexual prowess is admired in our culture; and addicts often have a type of "junkie pride" about their conquests, in which high intensity masks low sincerity. In her memoir, *Desire: Where Sex Meets Addiction*, Susan Cheever explains, "How is addiction to other people different from other addictions? In our world, addiction to other people—especially addiction to sex partners—is the only addiction that is applauded and embraced."[8]

Before his recovery, Larry, a successful middle-aged corporate attorney bragged, "My friend Mike is really jealous because he's not as good at it as I am," referring to his habit of picking-up young women at bars, health clubs, sports events, and other venues. "He can't figure out how I constantly attract women everywhere I go."

Also, as opposed to other addictions, sex taps directly into a necessary and extremely powerful biological life force—the instinct of sexual attraction, desire, and mating. As anthropologist Helen Fisher explores in *Why We Love: The Nature and Chemistry of Romantic Love*, there is chemistry involved in animal attraction that is the precursor of sex and human romantic love.[9] Sex addicts sometimes believe they have "fallen in love" during their many trysts, because it "feels" like it.

Greg, a high-level executive of a large company, spent over $500,000 on escorts before his wife discovered evidence of his secret life. He was considering divorcing his wife, abandoning his three children, and moving to another country to marry a high-dollar call-girl who was still "in the business." He scheduled a consultation with me to get an expert opinion about whether his feelings for the prostitute were "true love." In recovery, Greg began to realize that his feelings were the euphoria produced by the chemistry of a sex addiction, and that the prostitute was not "the love of his life" or his "soul mate," but a sex object who was an expert at making him feel special. Greg realized that what felt like love had caused him to do things he deeply regretted.

Cheever clarifies the confusion experienced by addicts like Greg, when she writes, "With human beings, how can we distinguish between passion and addiction? One primary characteristic of addiction is *always* a broken promise, whether it's a promise made to oneself or to another person."[10]

Warning Signs

Sex addiction is not just sex or sexual behavior that someone might find offensive or excessive. It is an illness, a brain disorder, characterized by specific symptoms—primarily, sexual preoccupation and compulsivity, and the inability to stop detrimental behaviors despite severe risks and consequences. Symptoms result from an addict's misguided efforts to self-soothe the discomfort of extreme emotions that he experiences. Some warning signs that sexual problem behavior may have crossed over into addiction are:

- Struggling to control sexual thoughts and behaviors
- Losing or impairing relationships because of the inability to stop sexual activities outside a primary relationship
- Lying about unaccounted for time that involved sexual activities
- Feeling guilty or shameful after engaging in sexual thoughts, fantasies, or behaviors
- Routinely pursuing sexual activities online
- Resorting to sex to escape, relieve anxiety, or cope with problems
- Losing time from work pursuing sexual activities
- Engaging in criminal sexual behaviors such as soliciting prostitutes, sexual harassment, or child pornography
- Participating in sexual behaviors that violate one's own values
- Blaming others for one's sexual behaviors
- Putting self at risk for STDs

Preoccupation, compulsivity, and loss of control may occur in many types of sex behaviors—fantasy, masturbation, pornography, affairs, the use of escorts and prostitutes, sexual harassment, exhibitionism, power-position relationships, anonymous sex, child molestation, and cybersex. Cybersex includes Internet pornography (iPorn), real-time encounters online or via mobile devices, soliciting or cruising online, and peer-to-peer sharing of sexually explicit material.

Addicts often report a "slippery slope" in which their use escalates and becomes more extreme in order to achieve the same "high." The iPorn addict may advance to images depicting violence and humiliation. The social media romance addict may cross over to more risky behaviors, such as web-camming real-time encounters or hooking-up for sex. The manager who is preoccupied with sexual fantasies may advance to seduction and serial affairs with co-workers.

The Costs

The illness of sex addiction is destructive and costly in many ways:

- Relationships, marriages, and families are destroyed when the promise of faithfulness is shattered by sexual acting-out and repeated relapses.

- Addicts may be fired and lose their incomes, reputations, professional affiliations, and credentials because of misconduct or criminal charges.

- Addicts may lose their freedom when they are sentenced to jail for sex offenses, such as soliciting underage girls online or downloading child pornography.

- Productivity is compromised at work when addicts are tired or hungover from late night computer sessions or other acting-out, or because they are distracted by their obsessions.

- Children and adolescents who are addicted to iPorn and use it as their model for relating, have long term difficulty with relationships, and often continue the addiction into adulthood (and add others) to make up for their intimacy deficits.

- Partners of addicts often experience symptoms similar to trauma survivors and sexual abuse victims, and frequently need their own therapy and recovery.

- Finances are strained because of spending related to the addiction—payments for phone sex, online subscriptions, prostitutes, hotels, gifts, and legal fees, as well as for medical expenses incurred for STDs, unplanned children, and counseling for addicts, victims, and their families.

- Children lose the guidance and nurturance of an addict parent who is preoccupied by the addiction, and of the other parent (if one is still around) who is preoccupied with the addict.

- Isolated addicts can become suicidal when they are trapped in acting-out cycles or when experiencing devastating consequences and deep shame or humiliation.

- Society loses the contributions of talented and experienced leaders who must resign because of sexual misconduct.

Roadmap for the Book

The Storm of Sex Addiction: Rescue and Recovery is organized into four sections. Each chapter presents vital information for anyone affected by, or interested in, this important subject. Part I, *The Storm*, introduces the warning signs of sex addiction and features the dynamics and nuances that are converging to create the epidemic. These include the cultural climate, the power of the sex drive itself, and the role of Internet pornography. Sex addiction is explained as a compulsive relationship with a mood-altering experience. Addicts substitute their addictions and intense-relating for real intimacy, because an addict is incapable of a close intimate relationship with another person.

In Part II, *Lost in the Storm*, I dive into an explanation of the forces that create an individual sex addict. The primary cause of sex addiction is attachment loss because of childhood trauma. I describe how maladaptive coping behaviors and buried memories from childhood emerge into the present and interfere with an addict's emotional functioning. Because an addicted person lacks positive adaptive responses to stress, he soothes himself with sexual experiences. He controls a source of comfort, pleasure, or power to avoid being engulfed in unregulated emotion. His sexual escapes become automatic.

I also explain how the excessive use of iPorn can lead to "self-induced trauma," a rewiring of the brain that disrupts the ability to have healthy relationships. Other curious aspects of the illness—the addict's "dark cave" of distorted reality, and the hidden dangers of undetected "companion addictions"—are also considered for their roles in the illness.

In Part III, *Surviving the Storm*, the hopeful option of treatment and recovery for addicts is presented. My Five Factor Wellness Model, which embodies the components necessary for predictable recovery, is outlined. By committing to this process, an addict can excavate his authentic self (buried by trauma), and reclaim the desire and ability for primary connections to be with people in healthy relationships, rather than with sexual substitutes.

In Chapter Twelve I address concerned partners who suspect a loved one is struggling with a sex problem. Partners need help with an assessment of their circumstances and with their responses to the revelations of betrayal. A confused partner often asks the question, "Should I stay or should I go?" To assist the partner with answering that question, "red flags" are listed, and the stages of increasing severity of a sexual problem—The Five Categories of the Storm—are outlined. By prioritizing her own wellness, the concerned partner can gain clarity and make healthy and rational choices about her unique situation. The problem with iPorn and sex addiction among clergy, a particularly vulnerable profession, is also presented in this section.

In Part IV, *Facing The Storm*, I present strategies to respond to the sex addiction epidemic. The first is the strengthening of family life—the best preventive medicine against addiction. There are Four Principles—Parental Connection, Protection, Respect, and Communication—that can provide our children shelter from the storm, equip them for building healthy relationships, and help protect them from iPorn and other social forces that can disrupt their development. Lastly, I envision initiatives that range from actions of personal responsibility to educational programs and society-wide intervention.

Ultimately, we must recognize that sex addiction and other severe intimacy disorders are not just the struggle of a few misguided people, but an emerging public health epidemic flourishing in a climate that is conducive to the storm. *The Storm of Sex Addiction: Rescue and Recovery* responds by providing what I hope is a useful primer on sex addiction and recovery for anyone concerned, but especially for addicts and their families.

CHAPTER TWO

THE STORM IS SURGING

Forces Driving the Epidemic

Sexual desire is the most all-consuming of desires. This desire is never sated, for the more it is satisfied, the more it grows.[11]

Leo Tolstoy

"Forty million Americans regularly visit porn sites. Do you know the clinical term for people who do this... Men!" quipped Jay Leno on the *"Tonight Show."* Our cultural sex preoccupation certainly gets laughs, but for many it is a dangerous problem that can cost addicts much that matters in life.

Just as multiple forces come together to create devastating hurricanes, earthquakes, and tsunamis, multiple factors are converging to unleash a virtual storm of sex preoccupation and addiction in our society. These elements are interacting, creating a context in which the storm can intensify while our defenses are eroding. Though the roots of sex addiction are usually found in childhood trauma, which is discussed in later chapters, there are modern variables and nuances that are influencing vulnerable people to make sex their drug of choice. Acknowledging there is a problem and understanding the confluence of factors contributing to this epidemic can help guide response strategies for treatment and prevention.

Factor One: Sex is the Ultimate Addiction

The first factor contributing to the storm of sex addiction (and underlying all other factors) is that sex is an extremely powerful natural force in-and-of itself. Sex is the ultimate addiction because it taps into a biological life force—the instinct of sexual attraction, desire, and mating—driven by the pleasure centers of the brain. Other addictions also activate the pleasure centers of the brain, but we were not born with an innate desire for gambling, alcohol, or cocaine. Interestingly, recovering addicts do compare the euphoria of cocaine to the euphoria of a sexual high, and find sex more similar to cocaine than alcohol in its addictive potential. They often suggest that recovery from sex addiction is more challenging than overcoming other addictions they have experienced.

Factor Two: The Internet

A second and more modern element converging to drive the epidemic of sex addiction is the ubiquitous availability of pornography on the Internet. iPorn is plentiful, cheap, and private. Most is just lurid, but some adds fear and aggression to supercharge the arousal. An infinite array of pornographic videos, images, and erotic experiences is accessible online. Such options have antiquated the feckless magazine.

Vivid pornography taps into parts of the brain that are designed to generate natural feelings of sexual attraction and desire for a flesh-and-blood person. But graphic images lead viewers deeper into a world of chemically charged fantasy, and further away from real relationships. Unfortunately, personal computers and mobile devices have become the primary dispenser of the ultimate addiction, expanding the number of porn consumers exponentially. iPorn is a gateway to more intense and risky sexual behavior, both on and offline.

Porno for Profit

With the Internet as a more direct and robust supply chain, the big business of pornography is fueling the epidemic by marketing sex as a standard lifestyle product. The quick-fix for loneliness, stress, or social inadequacy is sold like the latest household convenience. With low cost production and easy distribution, sex is commoditized and promoted as never before.

Pornopreneurs have created the Internet's most dominant industry, generating billions of dollars promoting their mood-altering sexual images and experiences. They have made great use of technology to attract the regular consumer and lure the casual browser. Every imaginable fantasy and experience is either mass-produced for the less discriminating, or tailored-to-fit and customized-in-detail for the more exotic tastes. Each consumer is special, and serviced with drone-like precision.

iPorn has become so prevalent that its use is often seen as unremarkable and even routine. But excessive use of porn may become irresistible and merely a portal to a more extreme fantasy or experience. Just as an alcoholic must consume more liquor to get the same effect, a step-up to the more extreme is required by a sex addict to attain the effect previously produced by milder enticements. The increasing tolerance and cravings sometimes drive pornography addicts into risky real life encounters. Some of the predators exposed on Dateline NBC's classic, "*To Catch a Predator*," could have been sex addicts stepping-up the level of risk and crossing over into illegal behaviors.

Ultimately, however, the iPorn industry can afford to be indifferent about people and does not require a grand marketing plan or successful PR campaign. Like the drug cartels, they are meeting a consumptive want. While vendors make the product alluring and available, it is sought-after and does a good job of selling itself. Slick marketing, the economies of digital mass media scale, and an eager audience combine to create windfall profits for pornopreneurs.

Do Not Feed the Bears

The Internet allows free and nearly unlimited access to vulnerable people. Not only are children reachable consumers of pornography online—where they get a front row seat at the virtual strip bar and can be up-close-and-personal to observe or participate in sexual acts—but also children can be contacted by highly skilled, well-rehearsed child molesters and pedophiles that may have a lifetime of experience grooming children into their influence. "Taking candy from a stranger" has entirely new meaning with the power of the Internet.

Women can also be stalked and targeted as sex objects, as addicts with character disorders and impulse control problems use social media or dating profiles to troll for their victims. Alarmingly, the Internet is fueling the incidence of more serious and criminal sex addiction disorders. More fish in the stream bring out more bears.

Factor Three: Sexualized Marketing and Media

While pornopreneurs specifically market their sexual wares, our society is awash in sexualized marketing, media, and entertainment in general. The sexual themes just keep getting bolder. And unless you live on a deserted island or under a rock, you probably know what I mean. TV, movies, music, and the Internet ooze with sex and innuendo. We have gradually been inundated and now sex occupies all spaces.

For example, HBO's "*Sex in the City*" was a breakout series that featured a probable sex addict, Samantha, whose shifting kaleidoscope of casual sexual relationships amazed her friends and buoyed the ratings. The short-lived MTV series, "*Skins*," had parents in an uproar as it titillated by glamorizing teenage sex. NBC's "*Parenthood*" followed suit with a scene of two sixteen-year-olds dropping their drawers to the floor in the show's season finale. So, more aggressive sexual themes have migrated from pay-cable, to cable, to network TV. Sex has a seeping stealth. Its advance is subtle and disarming, like cooking a frog by gradually turning up the heat, so it is not aware it should jump out of the pot until it is too late. Now, Lady Gaga can thrill with a crotch-shot as part of her live performance on "*American Idol*," and no one really notices or cares. And the most popular show on TV can be "*Jersey Shore*," whose "stars" made famous the subtle pick-up line, "Are you D.T.F.?" (Google-it if you need a coastal interpretation).

We have long been used to beer commercials, but now *everything* is marketed with sex—even bottled water. And everything is marketed with sex to *everybody*—products targeted to tweens and teens, such as body spray, cosmetics, music, clothing, and spring break travel packages are promoted with intentionally overt sexuality. Even younger children are exploited by age-compression advertising—the vigorous marketing of products and concepts that are age-inappropriate—that have a blatant sexual emphasis, such as dolls dressed like skanks, and video games that feature scantily clad characters.

Exposure that is "early and often" desensitizes children to the concept of sex. Immersion in sexual messaging and on-screen scenarios makes obsession with sex seem normal. It is no wonder that sexualized products and behaviors are irresistible to children and adolescents. It is normal for them to want to be more "grown up," but being grown up is labeled as "sexy" at every turn. Even iPorn is becoming accepted as cool among children, much like smoking cigarettes became suave in the 40's. As you know, it is not just cool to do it, but cool people do it! Constantly barraged by sexual themes, youth are more prone to sexualizing themselves and others and more likely to take sexual risks. Many children now carry a loosened sexual appetite into adulthood and learn to use sex to cope with confusing or complicated emotions.

Children or adults who have not withstood the onslaught of aggressive sexualized marketing and entertainment may have a distorted concept of self-esteem, and struggle through a series of disastrous relationships founded on over-emphasizing sex appeal and undervaluing other qualities. Sex appeal is simply not a stable basis for self-concept or relationships, but according to the merchants, it is pretty darn important.

Factor Four: Erosion of Family Life

The fourth factor driving the storm of sex addiction is the deterioration of the nuclear family and the erosion of traditional family life. A critical function of a family is to build a child's self-esteem. A child who is adequately nurtured and whose feelings and needs are validated will retain an important birthright—awareness of his own emotions and goodness—which is an excellent compass for navigating the adult world of relationships.

The bedrock of security, an intact family, is blasted from beneath a child by the trauma of ineffective parenting or divorce, and the child's ability to navigate relationships may be warped in the explosion. As a result of struggling or broken families, the important bonds between parents and children may be strained or severed. A child may have little sense of how it feels to be connected and secure in a loving relationship, and may not witness relationship-building skills modeled by healthy parents. Therefore, he may be confused about his own intimacy needs and have little notion how to achieve a satisfying relationship that nurtures emotionally and physically. Instead, the child may be learning that he is not worthy of attention and that needing others is dangerous and uncertain. He may conclude from experience and the aforementioned sexualized marketing and media, that sex, rather than intimacy, is his most important need.

Parents often underestimate their importance to their children and disconnect by having infrequent or critical contact. Children feel abandoned by parents who are distant or awash in emotional turmoil. Without the consistent reassurance and involvement of parents, children may conclude that any disruption or disaster is their fault, and that they are unworthy of commitment and love. This confusion is misguiding and leads them away from what they need—healthy connectedness—and toward the feelings of loss they have come to expect.

Even in intact homes, modern family life is an assault on children's self-esteem. Children are under-nurtured. Their time is either overscheduled or unstructured. They are often given more material things than attention, and are pressured to perform rather than play. Exhausted parents substitute fast food from the drive-through window for the family meal. They distract their children with tech gadgets and games, rather than engage them in conversation. Family time takes a backseat to children's peer groups out of fear that a child's popularity might slip. Parents' hectic work and social lives are conducted outside of the home, resulting in more solitude for the children, or in more developmentally sensitive time spent with unpredictable peers or technology.

These days, frazzled parents are irritable and controlling taskmasters, or conversely, relatively uninvolved, and children drift even further away from their abrasive interactions. Home seems to be the place to flee from, rather than the sanctuary a child needs. Many children wander lost in the wasteland of self-soothing with food, shopping, gaming, social media, relational aggression (bullying), substances, and sex.

Factor Five: Contemporary Cultural Attitudes

A fifth factor driving the surging storm of sex addiction is the shift over the last several decades into cultural attitudes of entitlement, immediate gratification, and excess. Everybody thinks they should get to have and enjoy everything with as little effort as possible. The quick-fix and easy-everything modus operandi promotes impulsivity as a virtue. Faster and lazier seems better. The joy of anticipation and the pleasure of savoring an experience, or the satisfaction gained from a sustained effort, seem amusingly old-fashioned. The same goes for relationships. Never mind friendship or courting—delayed gratification is passé. Fast, easy, and cheap has become a prevailing mindset, and it has seeped into our perspective on sexuality. This mindset lends itself to sexual acting-out, sexual excess, and sex addiction.

It is now considered normal personal choice to pursue lifestyles of excess with gluttony, greed, sloth, and sex. Every sociological and spiritual system warns of the disastrous consequences of overindulgence, but with the present cultural backdrop, which rewards the cult of personality over the development of character, an addict can easily maintain denial: "Everyone has it, does it, or at least they want to."

Factor Six: Autonomy and Personal Privacy

Expectations of entitlement, quick-fix, and excess become more toxic when combined with the historical American attitude that emphasizes individual autonomy and personal privacy. Sexual matters are usually considered "private." In general, this is good. But because of our high value on personal freedom, we sometimes stop short of naming reckless sexual behavior as anti-social, even though it creates serious social consequences. This allows us to cloak ourselves in societal denial about sexual problems. But many sex-related behaviors and activities generate considerable cultural expense, as well as heartache for innocent victims.

So is sex always just a private matter that should require our turning our heads? No. We must be cognizant of the darker aspects of sex hidden behind the veil of personal privacy and individual autonomy, so we can spot and heed warning signs that would otherwise be overlooked. Privacy should be balanced with awareness and lessened naiveté, and a willingness to act if there is trouble.

Consider the child victims of addictive families whose normal development is disrupted as a parent's illness robs them of attachment and security. Consider the collapse of marriages and family units, as sex addiction and divorce leave women and children in financial straits. What about victims of sexual predators or other sexually exploitive experiences? We cannot look the other way when coaches are taking young boys into the locker room showers, or girls are trafficked as prostitutes. They will struggle for years to overcome their wounds. And money is sometimes embezzled or obtained by selling drugs to feed an addiction. In fact, one of my clients was astonished when he reconstructed his expenses and estimated that over $250,000 (much illegally obtained) had been spent on his sex addiction over a period of six years. Needless to say, I was astonished, too.

An attitude overly protective of personal privacy has broader consequences when people are self-harming or inflicting harm on others. We must not bury our heads completely in the sand.

Factor Seven: Sexual Repression

Another factor driving the storm of sex addiction is the sexual repression and shame in our national psyche. Many of America's religious traditions carried (and some still do) a strong aspect of sexual fear and repression. Fears were derived from beliefs and teachings that suggested sexuality is sinful and shameful and should be kept secret. Sexual desires were considered impure. Sexual thoughts and behaviors outside the strictest definition of marriage were viewed negatively.

Shame and secretiveness about sexuality has been passed from one generation to the next and contributes to parents' reluctance to talk about the subject with their children. Such attitudes create resistance to providing human sexuality education beyond the mere essentials of reproduction. It remains difficult for young people to obtain good information about normal courtship and healthy sexuality, but poor information and ignorance abounds.

Many parents fear that providing education about human sexuality, including the stages of intimacy and methods of contraception, will pervert the morality of their children. They fear that it will open the floodgates and give their children permission to be sexually active. Parents also express concern that a sexuality curriculum would conflict with the family's religious or moral values, and they opt-out of educating their children about sex altogether. The topics of intimacy and sexuality can be readily taught at home or elsewhere, but most young people are provided little exposure to this knowledge. What better way to heighten curiosity and experimentation than to shroud a subject in secrecy.

Many of my clients have reported that if their parents said anything to them about sex, the mentoring was restricted to terse and cryptic communications like, "You know what happened to your cousin. Just don't be like her," or, "Don't do anything you shouldn't." Children quickly notice a parent's mutual discomfort with the topic of sex and relieve embarrassment by rolling their eyes and saying, "I know all that stuff," or, "I don't want to talk about it." Parents usually oblige the deflection.

Sexual shame and the resulting dearth of information create a high stakes gamble because no subject holds more curiosity or interest for children. We often take the longshot chance that they will manage to find good information on their own, but most youth glean their information from peers, media, and the Internet. This hodgepodge accumulation is usually poor and perpetuates myths and misunderstandings about sexuality and how to conduct successful relationships. Much of this *independent study* most certainly conflicts with parents' beliefs and values. Lack of information about responsible romance and healthy sexuality, combined with an abundance of false information, contributes to stalling or distorting the capacity for healthy intimacy.

Children require unapologetic nurturance that arrives in the form of information on a subject that impacts them deeply and intimately for life. If not provided because we are afraid, embarrassed, or ashamed, young people will seek and obtain misinformation elsewhere. Evasion of parental responsibility to mentor is part of the repressive aspect of the larger cultural dynamic. This affects our children's sexual template, and to an extent, underlies the cultural sexual obsession itself.

Factor Eight: The Sexual Revolution

The eighth dynamic in the convergence of sex addiction factors is a result of the so-called sexual revolution. The "liberation" from oppressive sexual fears, taboos, and gender roles that began in the 60's seems to have led to the trivialization of sex. Ironically, in an attempt to empower themselves by asserting control over their sexuality, many women self-sexualized and acted out, a faux empowerment that emulated and perpetuated the historical objectification by males from which they were trying to flee. This, aided by the disinhibiting effect of the birth control pill, created a more permissive sexual culture that allowed men greater access to sex, and resulted in women competing on an even grander scale for social acceptance and advantage based on sex appeal.

Furthermore, this social experiment—dissecting sex and romance from a committed relationship—overlooked the fact that it is difficult to split sexual intimacy from emotional and romantic intimacy. Sexual freedom and casual sex was believed possible and harmless, but the results have been marginal.

> *Sharon, a young sex and love addict, came to see me because she was depressed, having panic attacks, and so upset that she frequently missed work. She and her husband, Rick, started dating when they were fourteen. Both grew up in troubled families and clung to each other for solace. They married, but after a few years felt "something was missing." They began contacting other couples online and started "swinging," hoping that it would fulfill some of their desires or enrich their marriage. But this resulted in a great deal of confusion about who was bonded to whom, and for several years they struggled with complicated emotions about the couples with whom they were involved. They went through dozens of cycles, going to-and-from each other, and back-and-forth with other couples, swapping partners on a chaotic carousel of emotional unhappiness and misery.*

> *Another client, fifty-five-year-old Debra, had experienced many years of sexual freedom. She wept and flooded with shameful feelings as she told me a story of multiple partners throughout college, young adulthood, and mid-life. The partners were usually married men who lavished her with gifts and took her into their exciting lives of travel and exotic vacations. They also provided all the alcohol and drugs she wanted. Debra felt sad and*

ashamed for all of the lives that had been callously ripped apart by her capricious and compulsive sex adventures. She mourned the opportunities for meaningful relationships lost to years of promiscuity and a marriage to substances.

For these clients sexual freedom had been a rationalization for symptoms of underlying problems. Sex was merely a popular drug in circulation. While providing a thoughtless and convenient emotional escape, it built walls between themselves and the kind of relationships they really wanted.

Facing the Storm

In this chapter I have outlined some of the elements that are converging to create the epidemic—the *storm of sex addiction*. These elements include biological factors, such as the sex drive and the pleasure centers of the brain evolved to ensure procreation; technological factors, especially the widespread availability and use of the Internet and other social media; economic factors—the profit motives behind sexualized marketing, media, and the porn industry; and cultural factors such as the erosion of family life, and popular attitudes of entitlement, instant gratification, and excess.

Historical themes also intensify the storm. Because of the emphasis on individual freedom, the consequences of anti-social sexual behaviors are often ignored. A legacy of sexual repression and sexual shame leads to the avoidance of the topic of sex in our homes and schools; but naturally curious youth seek and find poor-quality and values-absent sex education elsewhere. And the sexual liberation movement that was intended to empower women and free people from inhibitions, inadvertently contributed to naive notions of harmless casual sex.

The storm of sex addiction is surging as these powerful forces combine to create an environment in which sexual impulses are misdirected and sex is becoming the drug of choice. Fortunately, most of us recognize that sexuality is intrinsically interwoven with the welfare of society, believe that reckless or impulsive sex is costly, and agree that sex should not be accepted as a commodity or a drug. And though we may have been lulled into a stupor by aggressive sexualized marketing and the widespread accessibility of pornography, most people still believe that healthy committed relationships are in the best interests of individuals and society. Therefore, we have the wisdom and the power to influence the expression of sexuality not for selfish and destructive ends, but toward respect for and the enrichment of life. It is because people instinctively sense what kind of connectedness they really need, we have a basis to ride out the storm.

CHAPTER THREE

SEX ADDICTIONS

Disorders of Intimacy and Intensity

*Addiction exists wherever persons are internally compelled to give energy
to things that are not true desires.*[12]

Gerald May

Sex addiction is about having a compulsive relationship with a
mood-altering experience because a sex addict is incapable of a close
intimate relationship with another person. Mood-altering with sexual
fantasy or sexual behavior is an addict's "fix" for deeply held fears of
inadequacy and vulnerability. A sex addict counterfeits intimacy and
may groom innocent victims who mistake an artificial love for the real
thing. The addict's purpose is to control another person as the source of
his drug, the intoxicating effect of which is often enhanced by power,
risk, or rage.

A sex addict often uses relationship partners or other willing sex
addicts as his suppliers. An addict whose particular addiction is
centered on "feelings" of romance and falling in love is essentially an
"experience" junkie who has learned to trigger a chemical response
in himself and a sex object. He choreographs the scenarios that
provide the fix. However, a sex addict is seeking intensity itself, not a

real relationship, and quickly moves on when his euphoria or sexual attraction subsides. Some addicts readily admit this fact; others are not so aware.

The intense feelings of sexual attraction or of being "in love" gradually diminish in normal relationships. Couples move from the euphoria of dopamine and serotonin inspired attraction to a quieter state of connection and bonding produced by the hormone oxytocin, which allows them to pay attention to something other than their sexual attraction.[13] Healthy couples progress through stages of deeper emotional closeness and enjoy the bonding experiences of stable emotional and physical relating. They revisit the romance phase of their relationship by sharing special times and places, but do not live in a state of euphoria and no longer expect to feel emotional or sexual intensity all of the time.

A sex addict, however, does not know how to get beyond sexual intensity to build a real relationship. He did not learn the requisite skills, and instead learned counterproductive strategies for close relating. The sex addict learned to mistrust others and to fear vulnerability. He seeks to control another person to feel safer and to meet his own needs, which precludes authentic intimacy. Trauma, including abuse or neglect in childhood, is the primary cause of such intimacy deficits. The arrested development of intimacy skills is acted-out in sex addiction and other closely related relationship disorders.

Learning Intimacy—A Developmental Process

An individual's ability to have healthy intimate relationships is based on experience—a gradual maturation of intimacy skills—a process starting at birth and proceeding in stages through late adolescence and young adulthood. The earliest intimacy skills are *noticing, attraction, demonstration of special abilities or accomplishments, flirtation, and romance*, first encountered in focused interest between parents and children. As parents and caregivers interact with a child and the child observes the parents interacting with each other, these complex skills are mimicked and mastered. If a child receives nurturing attention and his attachment to caregivers is secure, the child forms a positive sense of self and gains the ability to trust others.

As he matures, the child continues to experience a deepening of warmth and security with others by connecting through mutual sharing of thoughts and feelings. He learns that he is an individual, like others in some ways and different in other ways, and that differences are to be expected. He learns that needing affection is natural, and that touching is pleasant and reassuring. These additional skills of *mutual sharing of thoughts and feelings, individuality, and affirming touch*, learned in the family, are some of the same skills essential to building enduring relationships later in life. Normal socialization with other children and adults provides further opportunities for a child to consolidate his ability to relate to others. He learns that, "My needs are important and I can depend on others," and also that, "Others will connect with me, and both their needs and mine can be respected."

As a child's natural curiosity increases he becomes more aware of romantic intimacy—special feelings of attraction for a particular person. Girl and boy friendships, and dating that is free of sexual pressure, allow a child to experience emotional closeness using all of the skills previously learned. As an older adolescent or young adult moves into more serious dating, the skills learned in earlier stages provide guidance for making mature choices that respect both people in a relationship.

In healthy adult relationships, the skills described above can be observed as they are practiced in courtship. A couple may gradually advance to more emotional and sexual intimacy, progressing to stages of *foreplay, intercourse, and commitment.* In enduring partnerships, a couple experiences the periodic *renewal* of their relationship as they re-cycle through the stages of intimacy, and re-discover romance and commitment.[14]

If any stages of skills development are skipped by premature exposure to adult intimacy or erotic experiences, or by serious rupture of relationships with caregivers, a child's capacity for healthy intimacy in the future is in jeopardy. The ability to have relationships is experience dependent.

Most of us have not perfected our intimacy skills and struggle with various aspects of relationships. This simply means we are human. Struggling with sex addiction, however, indicates significantly arrested development at one or more stages that prevent an addict from having deep and fulfilling relationships with others. It predisposes him to having his significant relationships with mood-altering compulsive behaviors.

Types of Sex Addiction

The generally recognized types of sex addiction fall into ten categories of compulsive and out-of-control behavior.[15] The types of sex addiction often correspond to the intimacy skills an addict lacks, deficits that must be addressed if the addict is to have more authentic and fulfilling relationships.

The *fantasy* sex addict notices attractive traits in people and feels arousal, but lacks the social skills and emotional boundaries needed to interact well with others. He soothes feelings of loneliness and anxiety with masturbation and obsessive fantasy about an imagined world, but avoids real relationships. Fantasy sex is a principle feature of all types of sex addiction.

Voyeurism is essentially a one-sided flirtation in which an addict is saying, "You show me and I'll watch." It is an objectification of another person, and not a personal relationship. Arousal is experienced by viewing another person sexually, sometimes without her knowledge. Viewing pornography or erotic dancing, or watching others having sex, are examples.

With compulsive *exhibitionism*, an addict introduces himself in inappropriate ways to gain the attention and control he craves—"I'll show you mine, invited or not." He is often expressing eroticized rage by violating norms and breaking the rules, a misguided attempt at demonstrating his prowess.

In *seductive role sex*, an addict flirts or creates romantic situations for the purpose of obtaining sex, or for gaining power and control over another's feelings, not as an attempt to begin a real relationship, which is beyond the scope of his skills. His interest diminishes quickly after a sex object responds to the seduction. Rather than seeking a deeper relationship, the addict moves on to the next conquest.

Trading sex is also devoid of relationship. Arousal is derived from the sense of power that a targeted sex object needs something an addict can provide. The addict is willing to trade high-value favors or goods for sex. This often indicates childhood exploitation, a power imbalance with someone on whom he was dependent or should have been able to trust. As an adult, he has power of his own, and may be using it in a way that parallels his past experience.

Paying for sex with a prostitute, escort, masseuse, or dancer, is also a severe distortion of intimacy. An addict pays for pretend intimacy and illicit touch because he does not have the skills necessary to generate interest and romance in real relationships. The addict's powerlessness, rage, and humiliation, often deeply buried remnants of early life trauma, may be eroticized in an unconscious effort to overcome these experiences.

Intrusive sex is misguided touching and foreplay in which sexual arousal depends on violating boundaries without repercussions. An addict with this type of problem is angry or shameful and does not have the skills to develop a relationship in which touching is appropriate. The addict steals sex by touching in crowded situations, having unnecessarily prolonged physical contact, or "accidentally" touching breasts and genitals.

In *anonymous sex* no seduction is involved. It is just sex to get "high," sometimes intensified by the risk of getting caught. There is little emotional involvement because the parties are strangers. Anonymous sex is often the reenactment of loneliness, isolation, and shame, which are results of severe attachment loss.

Pain exchange sex includes sadomasochistic activities such as sex slavery, bondage, and asphyxiation, in which an addict's pain, degradation, or humiliation is eroticized. Compulsive behaviors of this type are often emotional or literal reenactments of childhood abuse, in which the child was treated in an emotionally or physically sadistic way.

Exploitative sex refers to criminal violations of sexual boundaries—preying on vulnerable people using force or seduction. This would include child molesters, rapists, and those who have sex with patients, students, congregants, or employees over whom they have power or authority. Sex addicts in this category often feign attraction, flirtation, and romance, or use their influential positions to gain access for sexual exploitation.

Compulsive Relationships

Patterns of compulsive relating that are often intertwined with sex addiction are codependency, romance addiction, love addiction/love avoidance, trauma bonding, and trauma repetition. In these disorders of intimacy, which may be found in sex addicts or their partners, emotional intensity is exaggerated far beyond what is typical in healthy relationships. The intensity is mistaken for love, and it too can be addictive.

Severe deficits in intimacy skills leave one vulnerable to these compulsive relationship disorders. Attempting to relieve an intimacy deficit, a sex or relationship addict relates to the emotional intensity itself as a substitute for intimacy, and is attracted to partners who will provide an ample supply of drama.

Codependency is a form of compulsive relating in which an addict avoids her own emotions by being preoccupied with another person. She may focus on another addict, partner, child, or parent to avoid her own shame about feeling inadequate or her fear of being abandoned. A codependent lacks the intimacy skill of individuality, and succumbs to the delusion that she can control, fix, rescue, or change others as a means of connecting and feeling valued. She may be so consumed with fixing others that she is numbed-out to her own emotional needs, and neglects her own wellbeing. When partnered with a sex addict, the codependent participates in unwanted sexual acts and enables the addict in order to preserve their pseudo-relationship.

A *romance addict* is addicted to the euphoric feelings of falling in love. She impulsively jumps over the early stages of relationship development and romantically idealizes a person whom she scarcely knows. Romance addicts often have a series of relationships in which they initially pursue aggressively and skillfully, but quickly lose interest.

A *love addict* also rushes intimacy in a desperate hope to find a partner who will love her unconditionally and meet all of her emotional needs. The love addict is attracted to a *love avoidant*, who participates in her speed-relating because he is aroused by the superiority of being idealized and the power of being needed. The love avoidant will soon begin to distance himself to evade the love addict's need for constant attention. The love addict will give chase. A pattern of jumping in and out of relationships with love addicts allows an avoidant to deny his own fear of abandonment and need for nurturance.

When a love addict and love avoidant pair-up, an extreme emotional roller coaster ride ensues. Their frantic episodes of pursuit, betrayal, despair, and rage replay attachment loss in early life. Dangerous cycles of splitting-up and getting back together occur. The two can even switch between the love addict and avoidant roles. Cycles may escalate into domestic violence, stalking, destruction of property, and other erratic behaviors.

In the *trauma bonding* pattern of relating, a person remains in or returns to a relationship with a partner who is emotionally, physically, or sexually abusive. Someone who is trauma bonded may be in deep denial about this reality. She does not expect to be noticed or to have needs of her own. She clings to her abuser in a state of confusion, panic, and despair, and to avoid the terror of being alone. If she finds the courage to leave she is likely to return, or attach to another abusive partner, unless her intimacy disorder is properly addressed. For example, Erin has separated numerous times from her husband of fifteen years, but always returns even though he constantly ignores, criticizes, and sexually humiliates her. She always believes that things will be better "this time."

In sex addition and compulsive relationships, partners stimulate super-charged brain chemistry to produce high intensity emotions, often an unconscious replication of early life experiences called *trauma repetition*. This is a pattern in which an addict unconsciously takes the role of a victim, perpetrator, or rescuer, and keeps his relationships in a state of disorganization and chaos, which replays the anxious unpredictability and insecurity in his early life.

The Intimacy Deficit

Many sex and relationship addicts know they have "problems with relationships." They often explain their situations in those very words, but they are confused about why they are having such difficulties. It is because they lack the skills for developing relationships and are substituting their addictions for real intimacy. They often view themselves as trying hard, but do not realize how counterproductive their efforts are. Some have given up on the effort to build deeper relationships altogether.

One's internal gyroscope for successfully navigating the world of relationships is developed through childhood and adolescence, beginning with emotional connection to parents and their modeling of loving relationships. Without solid intimacy skills, it is difficult to make sense of courtship, romance, and relationships. It is easy to get stranded and feel emotionally isolated. In this predicament, one is vulnerable to the illusion of instant relationships, and to using sex as a mood-altering drug, rather than experiencing it as an intimate communication of caring and commitment.

PART TWO

LOST IN THE STORM

CHAPTER FOUR

The Making of an Addict

Attachment Loss

Children who are not loved in their very beingness do not know how to love themselves. As adults they have to learn to nourish, to mother their own lost child.[16]

Marion Woodman

When I tell people that I have a treatment specialty in sex addiction, they often reply with something like, "Sex addiction... that sounds good, how can I get that?" While it is a humorous response, sex addiction is no laughing matter, and you certainly do not want to get it. But it does beg the question, "How does one get sex addiction?" What predisposes someone to getting trapped in the storm?

Attachment Loss is the Primary Cause of Sex Addiction

The primary factor that contributes to the making of a sex addict is *attachment loss* because of childhood trauma. Attachment loss is a profound sense of insecurity and loneliness, usually caused by physical, sexual, or emotional abuse, or by the literal loss of a caregiver—

experiences that deeply affect a child's ability to relate to people. At some point the addict as a child felt vulnerable and unprotected.

According to research by Patrick Carnes, a leading authority in the field of sex addiction, seventy-two percent of sex addicts were physically abused in childhood, eighty-one percent were sexually abused, and ninety-seven percent were emotionally abused.[17] As a result, when they were children they felt frightened and alone, were highly mistrustful of others, and lacked healthy skills for regulating their emotions—all of which placed them at risk for sex addiction because these and other disabling characteristics were carried into adulthood.

Many addicts also report that they felt desolate as children because family members seldom talked or played together, or parents were absent most of the time. Others were constantly criticized by their parents, who imposed harsh rules and showed little affection. Eighty-seven percent of sex addicts say their families were disengaged—that is, physically detached and emotionally absent. Seventy percent of sex addicts report their families were so rigid—autocratic, dogmatic, and inflexible—that the rules were more important than the child.[18] Often, parents in these homes are alcoholics or other types of addicts who are not dealing well with their own problems. Regardless of the source of attachment loss and trauma, children can come to feel that they are unsupported, unworthy of love, and must meet their own needs. How they learn to cope with their environment and life circumstances is what predisposes them to getting trapped in the storm of sex addiction.

Attachment is a Survival Instinct

If attachment loss is the primary cause of sex addiction, then the process of attachment must be pretty important. Have you ever heard of Owen the hippo and Mzee the giant tortoise?[19] Owen the hippo was separated from his mother when he was swept down the Sabaki River into the Indian Ocean and then forced back ashore as a tsunami struck the Kenyan coast. He was rescued by wildlife rangers and taken to Haller Park animal sanctuary. Soon after arriving, the less than one-year-old Owen proceeded to adopt a century-old male tortoise as a surrogate mother, with whom he established a strong emotional bond. Owen constantly followed Mzee around. He ate, slept, and swam with him. Sometimes Owen demonstrated protective behaviors when others approached Mzee. Strangely, the tortoise did not really seem to mind.

As one can imagine, this hippo has not developed exactly as he would have if reared by his natural mother. He has sustained substantial developmental damage. Even though the tortoise did his best to accommodate the strange situation, Owen has some unusual habits and behaviors, and if the opportunity arose, would have difficulty relating to other hippos—at least those that were not also raised by giant tortoises. So too, sex addicts—who have unusual behaviors and difficulty with real intimacy in adult relationships—grew up with abnormal or unhealthy circumstances.

The remarkable story of Owen the hippo illustrates the powerful instinct for attachment. The drive to survive by connecting is as primitive as life itself and is encoded into every cell of our bodies. For infant mammals especially, to be disconnected is to die. If unable to connect to a parent, a child or other mammal will connect to anyone or anything that floats by as a substitute. This incredible neurological programming encouraged Owen to attach to the tortoise for survival. Sex addicts, as children, also learned to connect to substitutes.

Baby mammals are hardwired to observe, imitate, engage, and attempt to emotionally connect to their parents. This flow of interaction not only ensures the youth's survival, but the relationship formed is also the anchor for the entire developmental process. Some illustrative research has been conducted that demonstrates how infants are biologically programmed to seek connection with parents.[20] It involved having the mother of an infant sit expressionless in front of a child. First, the child smiled and pointed to elicit attention. When this did not generate a response, the infant reached out and also tried clapping its hands. Because this too was ineffective, the infant looked around, made faces, and began to grunt and squeal. And finally, the infant contorted its body and cried in distress. An infant knows, at a feeling level, it must be connected to survive.

This need for attachment continues well beyond infancy. In a human child, the dependency period is far more extended than in any other species—at least twelve years or more. This allows for the development of a larger brain that is capable of more complex thinking. It also creates a long window of time in which a child's brain is vulnerable. Children are very resilient, but they are seriously damaged by physical or emotional detachment from their parents. Swept away from normal relationships with parents and caught up in an emotional tsunami, a child's survival mechanisms for connecting-at-all-costs kick-in. Much like Owen the hippo, a child whose healthy connection to parents is lost or significantly disrupted, will attach to whatever eases his pain—substances, behaviors, other people, or coping beliefs and fantasies that provide some comfort and shelter.

Childhood Trauma and Dissociation

When traumatized and disconnected physically or emotionally from caregivers, children must rely on their innate survival skills to cope with fear, anger, loneliness, and sadness. Because nurturing adults are not there for them, normal opportunities to learn positive ways to deal with emotions and to interact with others are lost. Traumatized children teach themselves to escape negative feelings by blocking them out or pretending they do not exist.

Children protect their fragile minds from overwhelming emotions through *dissociation*—psychological disconnection from thoughts, emotions, and memories related to agonizing experiences. They may become numb to feelings of rage, terror, despair, and to physical sensations of pain, in order to defend themselves from complete hopelessness. Dissociation often includes repression—the unconscious blocking, burying, and "forgetting" of painful memories. It can include distortions of reality—convincing themselves that their circumstances are "not so bad," or that they are "bad" children and thus deserve their circumstances, or that people hurt them because they "love" them.

Dissociation is a coping mechanism, a built-in security system that protects a child from feeling overwhelmingly hurt.

While detaching from their feelings, traumatized children are interacting and developing relationships with substitutes for the people who have not met their attachment needs. A substitute can be *anything* that eases anxiety and gives the child some sense of relief or control.

Fantasy

Sex addicts have a well-developed penchant for fantasy. This is usually rooted in childhood. Fantasy—dissociating by pretending—is a ready avenue of escape and comfort. Children's instinctive efforts to find something to calm or distract them from dire circumstances often begin with fantasy. They will invent fantasies to quell the terror of being alone and the rage from being abused. Imagination is easily accessible, a place where bad thoughts and feelings can be manipulated, shoved aside, or replaced with those directed and under the child's control.

When I first met my nine-year-old client, Annie, I noticed her twinkling brown eyes, graceful movement, and ready smile. I soon discovered that Annie had invented an elaborate fantasy world in which she imagined owning a new puppy to help her escape feelings of fear and anger. She had recently witnessed her father brutally assault her mother. The night of the attack, Annie overheard her mother question her father about evidence of his sexual affairs, and watched as he bludgeoned her mother with a chair. Annie feared he might do it again. Her mother brought her to therapy, but Annie refused to talk about the terrifying experience.

Annie was aware of the benefits of her imaginary world. She told me, "All the others are so upset all the time, but not me! I just threw all those problems in the trash and I think about my doggie." Annie was referring to a puppy she had seen at the local pet shop. When I asked if she would make a drawing of the puppy, she drew a picture of her fantasy world. She made herself and the dog, which she named Diamond, very large and central, while portraying the rest of her family as food in Diamond's bowl, and, apparently, they are also being digested and excreted at her feet.

At her next session, Annie continued to be preoccupied with the dog and again drew him larger than life, as the central figure, positioned protectively between Annie's father on one side and Annie and her brother on the other. She depicted her father as a towering stick giant, and her mother as a tiny, vulnerable figure. Annie gave herself a booming voice that demands, "Buy the dog now!"

At another session, Annie's coping skills were illustrated further when she drew a line of demarcation between herself and her family, clearly indicating she had separated herself emotionally. She depicted herself smiling, safe and happy, and astride her protective imaginary dog. However, she was facing away from her family, and Diamond's excrement was dumping on her dad, mom, and brother, indicating her disgust and anger. She also portrayed her parents engaged in a sword fight with her brother looking on, and added freshly prepared graves to the scene. Annie's desire to be happy, secure, and attached were on full display in her dog fantasy drawings, but so were her burgeoning fear, mistrust, and detachment. (See drawings by Annie).

My client, Clint, is one of the unfortunate sex addicts who were sexually abused as children. Clint was regularly taunted sexually and physically abused by his mother until the age of twelve, when he grew strong enough to push her away. She would force him to the basement, where she bared her body in front of him and ran his hands over her breasts. Clint was aroused by this and at the same time felt profoundly ashamed and enraged. Then because she had to "punish" him for his pleasure, she handcuffed him to a support post and beat him with a belt. He did not want his mother "to have the satisfaction of making me cry," and learned to numb himself out. He dissociated—psychologically disconnected from the horrific experiences—a coping mechanism common to many abused people.

Clint learned to mistrust people and to seek comfort in fantasies over which he had more control. With some embarrassment he told me that when he was little he invented imaginary friends and a pretend

world. "I called it Clintworld," he said, "and I had lots of friends there, kids that really liked me and were nice to me. When I was in Clintworld, my mother couldn't get me. My friends protected me."

Something Is Wrong So It Must Be Me

In addition to inventing fantasies to soothe feelings of profound loss, or to quell the terror of being alone and the rage from being abused, a child may develop a deep and pervasive sense of shame—a persistent feeling that her circumstances are her fault or that, "Bad things happen because I am bad." From a child's point of view it seems that, "Something is terribly wrong and it must be me!" In this way, she is dissociating by distorting her own identity. Unless she is reassured by caring and trusted adults that the situation is not her fault, and unless she is protected from further abuse, this can be the beginning of a lifelong distorted belief that, "I am not good enough," which therapists call toxic shame. Beliefs developed at the time of attachment loss such as, "I'm not good enough," or, "I can't trust anyone," are the warped lenses through which the trauma survivor views life and relationships.

Toxic shame is a dreadful burden for a child who has suffered trauma, because the belief that she is bad may become part of her identity. For the child it is not, "I was treated badly," but rather, "I am bad." It is not, "I was left alone too much," but, "I am alone." It is not, "My parents are hurting me," but, "I am not safe." And it is not, "Adults have most of the control," but, "I am powerless."

The role of toxic shame, as distinguished from normal shame, is particularly important as a precursor of addiction. Normal shame is a useful mechanism for self-correction that realigns one with one's values. This brings a sense of relief and reconnection with others by sharing the norms of behavior. But toxic shame is essentially contempt for the self—a profound sense that one's core being is unworthy and unlovable. This distortion also gives rise to the core belief: "I must not let others get close to me because they will discover how bad I am." Most addicts, who were abused or neglected as children, are haunted by toxic shame and run from it into addictive behavior, which only increases their shame.

Paradoxically, believing that a situation is "my fault because I am bad," which leads to the self-loathing of toxic shame, provides a curious form of protection. It allows a traumatized child the illusion of control because, "If it's my fault, maybe I can do something to make myself and the situation better." The child learns to meet her own emotional needs by steering the conduct of her mind. This survival response protects the child from the terrifying truth—that she has no power over her circumstances. However, a child's normal development is side-tracked by fantasy, shameful beliefs, and the illusion of control. She is left with maladaptive coping mechanisms that become obstacles in adult life and relationships.

Anything as a Substitute

The loss of nurturing attachment predisposes trauma survivors for sex addiction, because as children they learned to escape from feelings and to connect with something other than people for comfort. Children will attach to *anything* as a substitute, in order to escape, numb, or soothe feelings of profound attachment loss. If those upon whom children must depend are harmful, unpredictable, or absent, they will seek connection and comfort in behaviors and fantasies over which they have more control. If nurturance and security are not restored, children do their best to survive by finding ways to dissociate from the instinctive terror and utter hopelessness they feel. Traumatized children will detach from their own feelings.

These children do not learn what it is like to be connected well to themselves or others, a perception that is essential for healthy intimate relationships. They do not learn to share their thoughts and feelings, or to trust that others will care about them. Instead, they learn to be guarded, and to pretend that everything is okay, even if it does not feel that way. They learn to dissociate to avoid the deep emotional or physical pain of living in, or without, a family that has essentially failed them. Escaping from feelings becomes a familiar state. This predisposes them to becoming addicts who numb-out with addictive behavior. For those who have learned to eroticize their emotions, their mood-altering addiction involves sex.

CHAPTER FIVE

IT'S ALL IN THE PAST NOW, ISN'T IT?

Trauma Lingers

The ordinary response to atrocities is to banish them from consciousness.... Atrocities, however, refuse to be buried.[21]

Judith Herman

The person... in the grip of an old distress says things that are not pertinent, does things that don't work, fails to cope with the situation, and endures terrible feelings that have nothing to do with the present.[22]

Harvey Jackins

Trauma does not remain in the past. As Judith Herman states in her acclaimed book *Trauma and Recovery*, "Atrocities... refuse to be buried." A child who is abused or neglected is predisposed to serious and persistent emotional and behavioral problems because of the profound effects of trauma on development. Childhood attachment loss and the resulting repression of traumatic memories is a primary contributor to sex addiction because trauma refuses to be buried. It permeates the present life of adults in their inability to regulate emotions and their mistrust of others.

A successful entrepreneur and community leader, Stanley, spent several hundred thousand dollars on his sex addiction, trying to escape intense feelings of loneliness, a sense of not being good enough, and chronic rage. His wife and adult children experience him as critical, controlling, and arrogant. Throughout his childhood Stanley was beaten and humiliated during his father's frightening rages as his mother watched on helplessly.

The corporate attorney, Larry, has a shadow life of relentless romantic seductions and power-position relationships bordering on the criminal. He averages ten or more highly intense romantic or rescue relationships per year, often conducting them simultaneously. He feeds on a constant diet of admiration and adoration. Larry's father abandoned his mother and their children for another woman when Larry was four-years-old. His mother worked three jobs and still barely had enough to make ends meet. When Larry was eleven-years-old, his teenage babysitter forced him to have sex with her numerous times, and threatened that her boyfriend would beat him up if he told anyone.

Karen is a capable and attractive woman and the mother of three young children. She runs a small business and is the choir director at her church. Sadly, Karen leads a nonstop parade of paramours. She suffers from serious developmental trauma in which stress, such as her husband yelling at her, triggers flashbacks in the form of intense emotional memories of terror and of wanting to die. These were the emotions she experienced during childhood trauma, which included molestation by a family "friend." Her event-specific, visual memories of her sexual abuse are mostly repressed, but palpable emotional memories can manifest and erupt rapidly. Within seconds Karen can be in a fetal position on the floor of her closet, reliving feelings of wanting to die. Karen has been hospitalized twice for nearly fatal suicide attempts.

Stanley, Larry, and Karen are using sex addiction to escape inner turmoil and their behaviors are careening out of control. They long for intimacy but lack the skills to build healthy relationships. They struggle with unstable moods, distorted perceptions, and self-defeating reactions to stress. They are unaware that previous trauma is playing a leading role in their chaotic lives.

Repressed Memories

Repressed memories frequently intrude into the present lives of trauma survivors and interfere with their judgment. When we use the term memory, most of us are talking about normal memory, which is stored in a cohesive story-like form with images, sensations, emotions, and beliefs woven together. Normal memory gradually fades into the past. Traumatic and repressed memories have a tendency to linger around. They are splintered into fragments during overwhelming events experienced as a child. Images, sensations, emotions, and beliefs are torn apart. These disconnected pieces can later erupt into consciousness as separate "memories." These fragments may surface in the form of *explicit* memories, which are frighteningly vivid snapshot or video-like images of traumatic experiences; or they may surface as *implicit* memories, which include physical sensations, emotions, or beliefs that were part of the original traumatic experiences. When implicit fragments emerge into the present without an accompanying visually explicit memory, it is very hard to discern that these feelings of anxiety, fear, shame, rage, numbness, and loneliness are related to prior trauma.

Exaggerated Emotions

Current stress or the navigation of relationships triggers feelings lurking under the surface and cause addicts to overreact to present circumstances. They quickly launch into states of extreme emotion because they are stuck in survival mode—a persistent state of agitation, vigilance, and hyper-arousal—that leaves them full of anxiety and mistrust. They may even overreact to normal situations as if they were crises. Addicts unconsciously reactivate the feelings of prior trauma. This generates exaggerated emotions from which they want to escape. They may experience unconscious fear and rage about abandonment, abuse, or the deprivation of nurturance, or experience shame about not being "good enough." Addicts may feel terror rather than concern, despair rather than sadness, abandonment rather than normal loneliness, rage rather than anger, shame rather than disappointment, or numbness rather than anything at all.

The severe disruption of children's development damages their internal gyroscopes of true awareness of self and others. Attachment losses result not only in the inability of addicts to effectively regulate the intensity of their emotions (which are often out of proportion to current stress), but also in their tendencies to distort, misread, and personalize the responses of others. They may feel snubbed in an ordinary interaction, feel suspicion without foundation, or feel criticism when none was intended. Their mistrust leaves them feeling threatened or diminished. They may also disown their emotions, while attributing them to others. They often exhibit arrested levels of maturity in the form of self-centeredness or other immature attitudes. Ultimately, they try to soothe their emotional discomfort by dissociating and acting-out with sex.

Eroticized Emotions

Dissociating from emotions, a coping mechanism that an addict learned during childhood to help block feelings that were too painful, became an automatic response to intense emotions or stress in adulthood. At some point in his history the sex addict learned to escape his negative emotions by eroticizing them—turning them into sexual feelings—and acting them out in a disguised form, as compulsive sexual behavior. He lacked the necessary tools to deal with loneliness or fear or sadness, but there was something he could do about a sexual urge—get sexual relief. It became an emotional outlet. It *became* the coping mechanism.

Any emotion can be eroticized—grief, loneliness, rage, sadness, fear, and shame—as can feelings of stress or boredom. Commonly, a sex addict may escape from anger in the present by eroticizing rage and turning it into sexual feelings. A potent amalgam of furious feelings and misdirected sexual impulses, eroticized rage allows the addict to express anger buried at the time of the abuse. He can also feel strong and safe and avoid feeling dependent, which is now the dreaded unconscious reminder of painful abandonment in earlier life.

> *Larry, the corporate attorney, is a survivor of childhood trauma and a struggling sex addict. Larry abruptly walked out in the middle of his elaborate fortieth birthday party thrown by his three children, to call twenty-two-year-old Jennie, who is one of several current "girlfriends." Larry arranged to pick Jennie up and take her to a cookout at another friend's lake house. When she and Larry arrived, the host explained that the cookout had been postponed because his wife was ill. Larry was irate and curt with his friend about the change of plans, but had no remorse for bailing out of his own birthday party.*

In all likelihood, the birthday party set off a stress response reaction and Larry began feeling overwhelmed and out of control. He suddenly felt sexually aroused and proceeded to find his "fix," Jennie. Brushing people aside and displaying childish selfishness and entitlement in his activities with sex objects was a frequent pattern for Larry. His eroticized rage was evident because he was sexually aroused by "breaking the rules."

Family and friends of an addict may observe that his emotions are out of proportion or that his behaviors do not make sense, but are puzzled as to the cause. When questioned about his behavior, an addict may offer illogical explanations or rationalizations manufactured in his denial system. For example, Larry's reason for leaving the party was, "I was just bored and I knew Jennie would really enjoy the cookout."

My client, Clint, was sexually abused and physically beaten as a child. Clint took his anger to school and found a fight almost daily. Being a bully made him feel safer and in control. As a teenager he noticed the attention and admiration his brother received for "having a way with women." Clint soon added sexual fantasy and seduction to his repertoire. Now forty-three-years-old, he uses eroticized rage to control others, flaunt sexual norms, and "put one over" on partners by having a secret life.

Clint was referred to my treatment program by a friend in whom he had uncharacteristically confided (most sex addicts are secretive about their activities). He had a muscular build and exhibited a confident take-charge persona, but had come to see me in desperation—he had lost his second job because of sexual harassment charges, and an ethics review by the state licensing board of his profession was pending.

Clint told me he often felt like he was in "another world" when he was acting-out sexually. "I am not thinking about what I'm doing," he said. "Sometimes, it's as if I am not me." He was describing a state of suspended awareness, a form of dissociation. Clint destroyed numerous relationships, including his marriage, by having affairs and one-night stands. He confessed, "I was out to break every sexual rule I could think of, and I loved making women 'hurt' for me . . . at least emotionally." When he was acting-out he no longer felt angry; he felt superior and powerful. But his relentless sexualized conversations and behaviors at work had resulted in serious consequences. Even though his trauma may have occurred early in life, it continued to cause symptomatic reactions.

The story of Jane further illustrates the problem of buried trauma and eroticized emotions: A slender, attractive, soft-spoken woman of fifty-three, Jane is the director of social services at a large assisted-living complex. She ostensibly started therapy because she was depressed, overworked, and unhappy in her marriage. She stared at the floor as she described her inability to state her needs and wants to her husband, and explained that as a bright, liberated woman she found it embarrassing that this was so difficult for her. She began to cry as she told me that she had relinquished custody of her children years prior and no longer had contact with them.

But I soon learned that this was far from the whole story. In later sessions, Jane confided that she was inviting a married colleague home with her for sex when her husband was out of town. She had also searched for two former boyfriends on Facebook.

"I thought all of this was behind me, but it's happening again," she said.

"What's happening again?" I wondered. I listened carefully as she continued.

"I'm thinking about sex all the time. I'm acting really stupid." The source of her difficulties, her buried memories, gradually emerged as she told her story.

Jane had been very close to her beloved father, who was crushed to death in a tragic accident when she was nine-years-old. Jane does not remember crying at her father's funeral or any day thereafter, or talking to anyone about her sorrow. Her mother went into a deep depression, and because Jane was quiet and well-behaved, family members assumed she was doing okay. Jane went on with her life in a state of non-feeling typical of trauma, except for a sense that her father's death was somehow her fault. Without adequate reassurance, children often presume that unfortunate events are the result of their own misbehavior or bad thoughts. This sense of shame, based on their misinterpretations, can persist well into adulthood, as it had for Jane.

Jane began drinking in high school and it escalated through college and into young adulthood. Her life was focused on using "every imaginable substance," nightly partying, and engaging in frequent risky sex with multiple partners. She dropped out of college and worked various jobs or depended on her sex partners to support her. She was attractive and enjoyed the attention and power she had over men. "They needed me, but I didn't need them, and I liked that," she admitted.

Jane eventually maintained enough stability to finish college, and after graduation she dated a number of wealthy married men who lavished her with gifts and getaways. She had little interest in emotional bonds and preferred to be free to move on to the next partner. During those years, Jane rationalized her behavior as a lifestyle of "free-love."

Eventually she married, had two children, and her substance abuse dwindled to smoking marijuana several times a month with her husband. When Jane began graduate school against her husband's wishes, he filed for divorce and accused her of being a neglectful mother because she spent too much time studying and going to class. Because she felt guilty, she succumbed to her husband's accusations and gave him primary custody of their young children. He made parenting time nearly impossible for her and convinced the children she had abandoned them, so they refused contact with her.

Jane completed an MBA at a local university, where she also met and married another man. She felt deep shame about her past promiscuity and substance abuse and kept this part of her life secret from her second husband, fearing his rejection and abandonment. She also did not discuss with him the shame and helplessness she felt about giving up her children.

In therapy, Jane began to understand that acting-out sexually to escape from feelings was an old coping mechanism that reemerged under current stress in her marriage and work life. She began to grieve her childhood losses. She found a new job that was less stressful, and initiated contact with her children who were now receptive. Jane remorsefully revealed her infidelities to her husband, and gained the confidence to be more direct with him about her needs and desires. Their relationship eventually recovered. When I asked Jane if she still thought about having risky sex, she replied, "No, thank goodness, but think how close I came to wrecking my marriage, and what a waste that would have been."

Addicts like Jane, who banished feelings of shame, rage, or loss sustained in childhood, are unaware that their buried feelings are operating in the present and that they are using compulsive behaviors to escape from them. Driven by unconscious forces, the behaviors seem to take on a life of their own and often have a trance-like and robotic quality, as Jane described when she said, "During my years of drugs, partying, and sex, I really didn't feel much of anything. I just seemed to be going through the motions."

As we worked together to confront the early trauma of her father's death, she remarked, "I had no idea I was using sex to escape grief over losing my Dad." In one of our last sessions, Jane said wistfully, "Maybe if my mother or my grandmother had been able to talk to me about it, comfort me, tell me life would go on, that they would take care of me . . . things would have been different, and I wouldn't have done what I did."

Unfortunately, converting feelings to sexual urges that can be controlled and satisfied does not calm the feelings of loneliness or fear or any other emotions for long. An addict's attempts to escape with mood-altering, self-soothing sexual behavior, do not work. The buried memories of repressed trauma and the accompanying rage, terror, and shame, remain after the numbness or euphoria of the fix has subsided. Intense emotions, blocked to protect the hurt child, later fuel the sex that never actually satisfies.

Sex addicts have learned to erotize their exaggerated emotions so quickly that they are usually unaware of emotional causation, and are only aware of being sexually aroused. Addicts in recovery learn to recognize when they are using old coping mechanisms in current situations. They learn to slow down and notice the true emotions they are experiencing in the present, rather than act impulsively on sexual urges. They learn to respond to authentic emotions of sadness, loneliness, and fear in a more mature and esteeming way.

Precipitating Events

Another contributing cause of sex addiction is a stressful life challenge, such as losing a job, going through a divorce, or the death of a loved one. Precipitating events like these can plunge an Internet sex surfer, or a person with other problematic sexual behavior, into deeper water.

Consider Jim, a thirty-four-year-old computer technician, who came to see me after his wife packed her bags when she discovered his stash of Internet porn in hidden files. Jim hung his head and wept as he recounted what happened. "I looked at porn off and on for years. I thought it was what all guys did and not a big deal, but I knew Christy hated it, so I hid it."

In the previous year, Jim had gone back to school to finish a degree in computer programming and had a promise of a new job when he graduated. Jim was exhausted from working full-time and going to classes at night. His face flushed as he continued his story. "Four months ago, Christy had a miscarriage and I know we both felt terrible, but we hardly had time to talk about it. For some stupid reason I started looking at porn when I was supposed to be studying. Soon I was getting up during the night to go online when Christy was asleep. I even started looking on Craigslist for sex ads. I tried to quit but just kept obsessing about it and going back. Christy said she was suspicious because I was more grumpy and distant—and I was avoiding having sex with her. So she started searching, and it didn't take her long to find the files I'd tried to hide."

For Jim, Christy's miscarriage was a precipitating event. Like Jim, many addicts can identify an incident that pushed them over the edge, when their sexual acting-out ceased to be a solution to stress and became a problem instead. They may have previously used sex to relax or reward themselves or to distract themselves from unpleasant emotions, but they could put it aside when they needed to; it was not an addiction. However, under the pressure of a life challenge their behavior intensified and the addicts could no longer control their cravings.

I counsel people in predicaments every day in which stressful challenges overpowered their ability to cope and they began using sex like a drug: Under the threat of a layoff, the compulsive self-soother took up masturbating in the parking lot before work, putting himself at risk of getting fired before he could even be laid off. The sex chat-room user, worried about her father's Alzheimer's, doubled her time online and began hooking-up for sex with married men. The iPorn user whose wife filed for divorce started viewing more extreme forms of pornography, and was later arrested for soliciting a prostitute.

Trauma Lingers

Most sex addicts have unresolved childhood trauma that gets provoked by current life stress. Intense emotions, earlier blocked to protect the harmed child, later fuel the addiction. Those who have repressed rage, terror, and toxic shame about their dependency needs will engage in compulsive sexual behaviors, trying to rid themselves of their negative feelings. But sex does not solve their emotional problems. It never satisfies the truer need for attachment and intimacy in healthy relationships. Ultimately, addicts are being driven by the core beliefs, delusional thinking, and exaggerated emotions of which they are largely unaware—repressed trauma. And trauma refuses to be buried.

CHAPTER SIX

ESCAPE ROUTES

Neuropathways of Addiction

*Addiction is an illness of escape. Its goal is to obliterate,
medicate, or ignore reality.*[23]

Patrick Carnes

In a secure and nurturing environment, a child learns positive adaptive responses to stress through the modeling and guidance of caregivers. Healthy responses include connecting (with others who care); positive self-soothing; expressing one's emotions through healthy dialogue, interests, and activities; and responding to distressing situations by problem-solving. Children cannot sufficiently learn these "stairways to safety" if there is nobody to lead the way. As such, addicts as children did not learn these positive adaptive behaviors for emotional self-regulation.

Instead, children who experience trauma learn negative coping responses; they dissociate, numb, and have negative core beliefs. They carry these responses into adulthood as their reactions to stress. Stress triggers a re-experiencing of their trauma—which refuses to remain buried—and their coping responses are automatic. Mardi Horowitz termed these reflex-like reactions, the *stress response syndrome*.[24]

This helps explain the bizarre behavior of sex addicts. Their brains are hijacked by memories of trauma, their emotional responses are spontaneous, and their self-medicating actions are impulsive and lack adequate forethought. They live in a chronic state of hyper-arousal in which exaggerated emotions compel them to seek an escape. They escape by compulsively arousing and soothing themselves with sex.

An addict appears to be making deliberate choices when he is acting-out, but he has actually lost control. He has been programmed to automatically attempt to regulate his emotions sexually. This habitual sexual "doping" has forged an arousal template in the addict's brain—a consistent and reliable pattern of mind-altering escape. But it is not merely a psychological escape—it is biological, and chemical. Neuropathways in the brain are physiological "escape routes" that an addict uses when he feels overwhelmed. Like lighting a fast fuse, these neuropathways are strings of chemical transmitters that when stimulated by sexual thoughts or behaviors, provide instantaneous relief by producing sensory and emotional experiences of fantasy, arousal, numbing, or deprivation.[25]

Escape Routes—Neuropathways of Addiction

The adaptive child learned to activate these escape routes of fantasy, arousal, numbing, and deprivation to dissociate from the overwhelming emotions he or she experienced during trauma. A poignant example of a child's innate protective ability to stimulate the neuropathway of fantasy is depicted in a famous photograph by David Seymour, *Children Playing with a Broken Doll*, taken in Naples, Italy in 1948. In this photograph, the adoring gaze on the little girl's face suggests her fantasy has eclipsed her war-ravaged surroundings. She is transported out of her poverty, and she does not care that the doll she holds has no head, arms, or feet. She is imagining it as she needs it to be, and the little friend next to her seems to be happily caught up in the pretend as well.

At some point, having learned to unconsciously eroticize strong emotions, an addict has sexualized the neuropathways of fantasy, arousal, and numbing, which provide a programmed sexual response to intense emotion. Without conscious effort, the addict mainlines his sexual drug directly to the pleasure centers of his brain. As he repeatedly uses sex and activates his neuropathways, a tolerance develops. Larger doses of his sexual drug are needed to produce the same emotional effect. This requires increasing the risk, intensity, or frequency of sexual behaviors. Most addicts combine, alternate, and cycle in and out of their use of the neuropathways.

Fantasy, Arousal, Numbing, and Deprivation

The first escape route is the *fantasy* neuropathway. Fantasy is central to all sex addictions in the preliminary obsession, preoccupation, and ritual stages of acting-out. A sex addict usually has a governing fantasy that transports him to the imaginary world of his preference to avoid discomfort in his real life. The governing fantasy is part of his sexual arousal template and often has its roots in negative early sexual experiences. Almost any thought, behavior, or object can be eroticized and woven into the sexual arousal template if it carries sexual meaning for the addict.

The second escape route is the *arousal* neuropathway. To avoid unbearable emotions for which he has few positive adaptive tools, a sex addict learns to stimulate the neuropathway of arousal. He escapes by creating strong feelings of sexual pleasure, power, or danger using intense sexual fantasies or by engaging in high-risk sexual behaviors. For many addicts the arousal is enhanced by eroticized rage in which they consciously or unconsciously take revenge against a parent or spouse by violating sexual norms, such as having sex in dangerous places or with inappropriate people.

An addict may also avoid unbearable feelings by stimulating the neuropathway of *numbing* with calming behaviors, such as browsing pornography online or compulsive masturbation. He may combine sexual behaviors, either simultaneously or in serial fashion, with alcohol or other sedatives, or with other numbing behaviors such as overeating, endless web surfing, or mindless gaming.

An addict sometimes uses multiple behaviors to arouse and numb, depending on what is required to get temporary relief. For example, eighteen-year-old Kate would spend hours cruising the Internet before going to a party to get drunk. She would then hook-up for sex with strangers she met online. She packaged the behaviors of arousal and numbing because they combined to facilitate her needed escape.

The fourth escape route is the *deprivation* neuropathway. Because addiction is usually associated with the use of substances or behaviors, it is difficult to understand how deprivation can be a part of addiction. However, addiction has a flipside, an opposite extreme of compulsive avoidance. Deprivation is a neuropathway that addicts learn to activate by withholding from sex (or other things, such as food) in an extreme way. Withholding can release brain chemicals that produce a sense of relief and even euphoria. An addict can feel in control, superior, and safe by blocking feelings of need and want, and in this way deny any frightening dependency on others.

Chaotic Relationships and Negative Emotions

Chaotic relationship patterns such as codependency, romance addiction, love addiction/love avoidance, trauma bonding, and trauma repetition can become addictive and often co-exist with sex or other addictions. With these coping behaviors, which manifest in relationships, an addict unconsciously recreates intense feelings while interacting with other people. The addict is unable to stop what have become programmed patterns of intense relating, even though the drama is very evident. These high intensity patterns of relating can stimulate the neuropathways of addiction.

Negative core affect states—toxic shame, rage, self-loathing, despair, and depression—can become addictive as well. Negative core emotions can be very intense and consuming. Dwelling in negative emotions becomes another means of escape from the present. These high intensity emotional states may also co-exist with sex or other addictions. They are easily evoked in trauma survivors and can likewise stimulate the neuropathways of addiction.

Programmed to Escape

For a sex addict, "jumping out the window" into his addiction and acting-out with compulsive sexual behaviors, is the alternative to enduring the unregulated emotions of unresolved trauma, which can otherwise leave him awash in intense feelings or acting desperately in his relationships. When an addict feels he is about to be engulfed by emotion, it seems to make intuitive sense to escape. The addict repeats the programmed "escape routes" by stimulating neuropathways with sex. He is not thinking about consequences, only the escape.

Sex addicts generally have no idea how old the scripts are in the stories of their lives. Their thinking and patterns have become so engrained that their chemistry has been altered. They have developed a brain disorder. This is certainly no excuse for addictive sexual behavior. In fact, with this knowledge an addict should hold himself accountable to seek treatment for his problem, as he would with any other serious illness. Recovery is a process by which an addict can restore healthier brain functioning by learning positive coping skills to better regulate his emotions. It is a challenging process of learning who he is, where he is, and that he has real choices about how he feels, experiences self, and behaves in the present. He can reclaim his capacity for intimate, loving relationships.

CHAPTER SEVEN

INTERNET SEX ADDICTION

Lightning Strikes

At the center of every addiction, as at the center of every cyclone,
is a vacuum, a still point of emptiness that generates circles
of frantic movement at its periphery.[26]

Peter Trachtenberg

Childhood trauma and attachment loss can put people at risk for becoming dangerously addicted to sexual stimulation. But there is another more contemporary and potentially more hazardous contributor to the storm of sex addiction. What I have termed *self-induced trauma* is caused by overexposure to Internet pornography and its accompanying social and intimacy isolation. This relatively new phenomenon is an ominous mutation of the etiology of sex addictions. The potency and accessibility of online pornography is an intensely addictive outlet for anyone who struggles with a sense of disconnection. Add sexting, cruising for sex online, the sharing of sexually explicit material, and with the touch of a screen, no one need feel lonely or unlovable anymore. Even the shyest or most reclusive man or woman can shed all inhibition and engage in sexual adventures they could only have imagined in their dreams.

.The Internet offers instant access to mood-altering experiences in a setting of privacy, convenience, and affordability.[27] Sites and services are so plentiful, and the apparent need for this addictive escape so unbridled, that iPorn has been called the "crack cocaine of sex addiction."[28]

The Internet is open 24/7 to indulge an addict's every fantasy, and this immediacy is hazardous because it plays into impulsivity. Online there is only a small window of think-time between impulse and action. The intensity of the images and the hypnotic quality of the experience impair judgment. For a sex addict, having Internet access is comparable to an alcoholic hanging out in a bar twenty-four hours a day, or a drug abuser living in a pharmacy. Oftentimes, substance abuse goes hand-in-hand with Internet related sex addiction; however, therapists are seeing a greater number of sex addiction clients with no history of substance abuse, or even childhood trauma, as predisposing conditions.

High potency visual images, illicit sexual or romantic conversations online, and web-camming sex acts, hijack the neuropathways of fantasy and arousal, repeatedly targeting and tapping directly into the pleasure centers of the brain. This causes dysregulated brain chemistry, and the iPorn junkie loses the ability to make healthier choices. He becomes increasingly withdrawn from the world of real relationships. Looking at Internet pornography can quickly become an uncontrollable toxic habit, which may soon lead to marital crisis, legal charges, and public humiliation. Regular sexual activity via the Internet leaves a trail of incriminating erotic evidence.

Consider Dean, a senior law enforcement officer, who grew up in a loving family in a pleasant suburb and is still close to his parents and two brothers. Dean might drink a few beers, and he tried marijuana a few times in college, but he never had an addiction, not even to TV. However, as soon as Dean began using the Internet, he was hooked. He found himself rushing home in the evenings to get online—logging on to Facebook, checking out his stock portfolio, and pouring over blogs on everything from exotic travel to the latest exercise fad. Often, Dean would look at his watch and be surprised that hours had passed since he had turned on the computer. His focused attention and immobility was conducive to a trance-like state, a condition in which people are more receptive to suggestion.

For Dean, the tipping point came when he decided to browse a few porn sites. Within weeks he was in the zone, looking at porn more than four hours every day. His brain was stimulated by arousing images, sounds, and words, without the filtering that normally occurs when a person is fully alert. His thinking, judgment, and values were set aside as he became absorbed in the experience—essentially mainlining the arousal directly to his brain.

Dean soon preferred his Saturday night dates to be with iPorn, but he also checked out dating sites and began several impulsive sexual relationships. His hook-up and intense affair with a married woman became an obsession that lured him into illegal behavior—stealing confidential information for her from an agency's files to which he had access—to "prove" his devotion. In a matter of months Dean lost his job, his professional credentials, and many of his friends who had warned him to stop seeing the woman.

Heavy consumers of iPorn, like Dean, often combine the erotic euphoria of pornography with masturbation, continue to increase the frequency of their viewing, and later step-up to more extreme forms of online sex and related behavior—just as substance abusers increase their use or move on to even more potent and dangerous drugs. Those that become sex addicts soon find their cravings so hard to resist that they risk everything for a sex fix. That is what happened to Dean.

Addicts ultimately put themselves and their families at risk, as did my client Teresa before she sought help. Women tend to be more secretive about their online sex activities, and more likely to act-out their behaviors in real life, such as having casual sex, multiple partners, and serial affairs.

When Teresa called for a consultation she sounded desperate. "Please, I have to see you as soon as possible," she pleaded. "My husband told my entire family that I am having an affair and now they are blaming me for all of our problems. He is filing for divorce and wants custody of the kids."

Teresa's husband had become suspicious and had done some investigating. He confronted her after he found sexy lingerie tucked away in her closet and discovered her secret email account.

At her first appointment, Teresa cried as she told me that she had confessed to her husband that she had slept with one of her old boyfriends. "But, there is more, a lot more." She shook her head and continued, "I first started chatting with guys online. I was a little flirtatious and it was fun. Then it got more suggestive, and eventually, I met several of the guys for sex. Soon I was daydreaming all the time about the next romantic lunch or night out."

She paused to wipe her eyes with a tissue, then started again. "My husband has done very well with his companies. He has offices all over the world and we've moved the family several times so we could all be together. But for what? He is still gone most of the time on business trips." Now she was sounding more angry than sad. "I guess that's why I got involved with chatting. It was exciting and it felt good to be special to somebody, but it went way too far."

Teresa had mistaken the pseudo-intimacy of her online encounters for the intimacy of a real relationship, and it tempted her into offline sexual affairs.

She put her hand over her eyes and started sinking into feelings of guilt and shame. "I've wrecked everything and my husband was just trying to give us a good life."

Nobody Will Know

The illusion of Internet anonymity—that "nobody will know"—reduces inhibition. The careless Internet user may wander deeper into the lonely labyrinths of the web, and learn too late that what is launched into cyberspace can never be reclaimed. What seems like private behavior can lead to public embarrassment, legal jeopardy, and marital disaster, as it did in the following case:

Tim was absolutely humiliated when he was arrested in an online sting operation and his name appeared in the local paper. He explained that he came for a consultation with me because his doctor thought he was depressed and possibly suicidal. "But I don't think there is any way you can help me," he said.

He began to talk about his arrest and how his problems had started. Speaking in a near-whisper, Tim said, "After I lost my job, about ten years ago, I felt like a total failure. My wife was really angry about it, so we argued sometimes and that just made me feel even worse. I had nothing else to do, so I messed around on the computer. I looked at some porn, you know, stuff I had heard about from different guys."

"And what happened after that?" I inquired.

Tim winced as if I had stabbed him, but then continued. "I had always been curious about escorts and so I started checking out sites and thinking maybe I could meet a couple of the women I picked out. I finally met one girl for sex, but I felt terrible afterwards. I went back a few more times, and then it got to be a regular thing."

I asked Tim how long and how often he had been seeing prostitutes.

"Weekly or so for about eight or nine years," he said. "I was so ashamed. I really did everything I could to keep it to myself." Tim looked directly at me and said, "I've never talked to anyone about this, but I've got to know—am I just plain crazy?"

Tim's wife, Allyson, accompanied him to our second session. She was a picture of courage under fire with her chin up, shoulders squared, and an expression of stoic determination on her face. Allyson described her shock when her brother had called and told her that Tim had been arrested for hiring a "hooker" online. "It didn't sink in for a while. I just thought it was some mistake. But then I started to feel sick, and now I'm furious! I know he's in big trouble, but does he have any idea how I feel," she said glaring at him. "The whole world thinks my husband's a cheating pervert, and I look like a fool!"

People have a tendency to explore their hidden fantasies if they think they are undetectable. But presuming Internet activity is anonymous and does not leave a trail of incriminating evidence is comparable to a two-year-old putting his head under a blanket and thinking nobody knows where he is. The Internet user who forgets that Internet anonymity is an illusion, is taking his chances.

Infinite Opportunity

Another hidden liability of the Internet is the boundaryless nature of the online experience. This techno-version of, "What's over the next hill?" adds to the seductive power of the Internet and to the development of addiction. There is always another online friend to chat with, or a more risqué porn site to explore. The never-ending quality and infinite opportunity of the Internet is dangerous, because the pleasurable effect of a process that does not come to a close can be like a stimulating drug or a sedating trance. These sensations are especially seductive to people who are troubled and escaping their emotions.

Another client of mine, Jason, said that sex online was "the best drug ever," and that he never considered how dangerous zoning out in front of the computer could be until it was too late. He described how terrified he was when agents from the Interstate Commerce Enforcement Agency and FBI pounded on his door in the middle of the night and confiscated his computer.

"My wife, Amy, started screaming because agents swarmed through the house with guns like a SWAT team," he told me. The agents arrested Jason on charges of possession of child pornography, a felony offense. Jason's voice trembled as he described nightmares in which he is being transported to prison in a police car. "I just don't know if I can face this," he said.

Jason told me his problem began when he started viewing online pornography to fulfill his sexual cravings without really "cheating" on his wife. In a few months, Jason was spending every available hour scurrying from one porn site to another. "And that was even before I got involved in the young girl stuff," Jason added. "It felt pretty sleazy at first, but exciting, too, and I kept going back for more."

Jason was spellbound by the limitless opportunity to look at porn without anyone knowing—or so he thought. Jason's addiction progressed to illegal behavior, as his judgment diminished.

Virtually Alone

Another insidious hazard of the Internet is its isolating and depersonalizing effect. Relating to people is replaced with relating to a transaction. The human element is constricted or completely absent. There is a richness of personal interaction that is lost online—merely talking to friends is accomplished by some form of messaging, rather than by having face-to-face conversations.

My grandmother used to cross the street each day and visit her friend, Mabel, who was not getting out much in her later years. Grandma would take me along and we might bring flowers from the garden, fresh bread with honey, or a book to share. Mabel always greeted us with a big, "Hi, there!" and hugs. The women would chat about the news or the local happenings, or sit quietly together and do needlework. I played with toys nearby or just listened and soaked in the warmth of their friendship. I think their visits would not have been the same by text or email, nor would my memories.

But maybe that is a little old-school. I certainly understand that people now develop important emotional attachments through social media. But while such activities may meet needs for interaction, they require little effort and carry a lower risk of rejection. They are far less emotionally threatening than real-life situations. Online experiences may feel intimate through the screen, but it is a pseudo-intimacy, a risk-free substitute that may actually impair a user's ability to relate to flesh-and-blood people. Healthy relationships require refined social skills, interpersonal risk, sustained effort, and adequate face-time. The vast difference between a real relationship and a virtual one, may be compared to being in Hawaii with someone special, or just getting a postcard that says, "Wish you were here."

The Internet Ambush

I have heard enumerable stories from people who left the confines of their computer to meet an online partner in person and were dismayed and disappointed when they discovered that he or she was ten years older, one hundred pounds heavier, or married rather than divorced. Which begs the question, "Why do people pretend to be someone else on the Internet?"

The short answer is, "Because they can." Some pose online to experiment with how it feels to be a different person, a stunt that is difficult to pull off face-to-face, but easy to do on the Internet. As a *New Yorker* cartoon declared, "On the Internet, nobody knows you're a dog."[29] Others pose because they have low self-esteem, poor social skills, or want to deceive and exploit people. Online communication lends itself to treating others like objects, and to filling in the blanks of missing information with fantasy for personal gratification. For the poser, even if a quasi-relationship begins to form, the recipient is not responding to an authentic person, but is being tricked into relating to a pretender. The fantasy bubbles are destined to burst.

So what about claims that the Internet is a good place to meet a partner? Can an online relationship be successfully migrated offline? To be sure, if an online introduction blossoms into a real-life coupling, that is great. I know plenty of people who have dated successfully online and have even found spouses. It is the initial fantasy, unrealistic expectations, potential for posing, and lack of intimacy that are concerning.

Internet Use Warning Signs

Excessive use of the Internet can be hazardous to one's health and wellbeing, especially when one is tired or lonely or angry. Cruising the back alleys of the Net is asking for trouble, and doing it late at night is especially dangerous. Unfortunately there are no "bartenders" online who refuse service if a patron has had too much. There is no manager who scoots shoppers out of the store. There is no ref who calls "game-over," and no parent who says "nighty-night." There is, instead, a plethora of master salespeople skilled at trapping vulnerable users, and there are countless predators soliciting lonely singles, discouraged partners, and curious children.

Bob, a forty-three-year-old high school teacher in recovery from sex addiction, mentioned that his son, Brian, was "staying up late at night doing stuff on the computer. He's getting to school late and falling asleep in class." I suggested Bob explore further to determine exactly what Brian was doing online. Bob discovered that Brian was not only chatting with friends, but also engaging in sex-talk with several girl "friends," web-camming suggestive activity, and visiting porn sites. Brian was on his way to a serious problem before his father intervened.

Chris, a nine-year-old boy, was not as fortunate. Chris discovered iPorn while playing computer games and within weeks he was viewing and masturbating compulsively. His parents were preoccupied with the collapse of their marriage, so Chris was often unsupervised. His sexual behavior escalated and by age twelve he was charged with sex offenses against neighborhood girls as he acted-out what he saw online. He was sentenced to a treatment facility for youth offenders. At age sixteen his sex addiction was finally diagnosed, just before he was incarcerated again for further offenses.

Spending more than twelve hours per week online in "entertainment" activities is often an early sign of trouble. Internet use at this level compromises other areas of an individual's life, such as family time, employment or school productivity, face-to-face socialization, exercise, and sleep. Criteria for problematic Internet sexual behavior have been established by experts and are as follows:

- Preoccupation with sex on the Internet, such as having

obsessive thoughts about the previous online activity or anticipation of the next online session

- Going online more frequently or increasing amounts of time online in order to achieve satisfaction

- Increasing the intensity or risk of online sexual experiences

- Repeated, unsuccessful efforts to control, cut back, or stop using the Internet for sexual purposes

- Feelings of restlessness, moodiness, depression, or irritability when attempting to cut down use

- Staying online longer than originally intended

- Jeopardizing or risking loss of significant relationships, job, educational or career opportunities because of Internet use

- Committing illegal acts online or incurring financial consequences for online sexual behavior

- Lying to family members, a therapist, or others to conceal the extent of Internet involvement

- Using Internet sex to escape from problems, or feelings such as hopelessness, guilt, anger, anxiety, and loneliness.[30]

Cyber-safety

Like the enchantment of the Siren's song called ancient sailors to their deaths on the rocky shores of Greece, the Internet can lure the unsuspecting traveler into the dark and dangerous cyber-world of sex addiction. To avoid calamity, we must be aware of safety and moderation in our own use of the Internet and that of others in our homes.

People who have addictive disorders, and those who are isolated, marginalized, traumatized, or young, are more susceptible to the enticement and potential harm of the erotic euphoria of cybersex; however, adults who have no apparent history of addiction or trauma are becoming compulsive users as well. They can sustain self-induced trauma and become addicted by excessive exposure to imagery and intensity that overwhelm brain functioning.

The Internet has enormous capacity for enhancing our lives, but it is driving the storm of sex addiction because the very attributes that make it so useful have uniquely addictive potential, and can have harmful effects on social development. Safe and responsible use of the Internet is a public health issue that demands our concerted efforts to prevent further casualties. Just as our fire-making ancestors did, we can learn from our mistakes, enjoy the benefits of this immensely powerful technology, and take measures to safeguard against the dangers.

CHAPTER EIGHT

THE ANATOMY OF THE STORM

The Addict's Dark Cave of Distorted Reality

Problems cannot be solved at the same level
of thinking that created them.[31]

Albert Einstein

To fully understand sex addiction and how to recover from or prevent it, it is imperative to first gain a grasp on addiction more generally—to recognize the stormy *addictive system* of addicts.[32] The commonality in all addictions is that they include delusional thinking and cycles of irrational acting-out behavior. The delusional thinking involves negative core personal beliefs and mechanisms of denial. When these elements are coupled with life stress, addicts plunge into cyclical patterns of preoccupation and ritualization related to their addiction, followed by engagement in their addictive behaviors.

After acting-out, addicts typically feel despair as their lives become more chaotic, which in turn reinforces their negative core beliefs and provokes their mechanisms of denial. Addiction is essentially a bad feedback loop—a circular pattern of thinking and behaving—that keeps addicts trapped in the storm of their addiction. With each new plunge through the acting-out cycle, an addict's problem gains momentum and increases in severity. To effectively combat sex addiction, we must attack the delusional thinking. (See diagram, *The Addict's Dark Cave of Distorted Reality*).

The Addict's Dark Cave of Distorted Reality

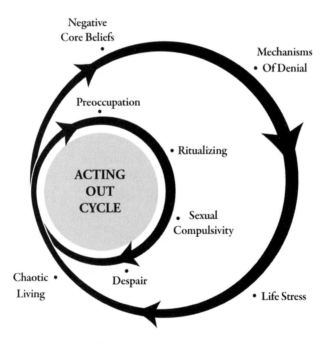

Delusional Thinking

I want you to pretend you are in a cave. It is completely dark. You can see nothing. It is starting to flood. There are twenty-five howling, drooling werewolves, and fifty glaring, hissing, incredibly thirsty vampires surrounding you. What would you do? I often ask my clients this riddle, and they invariably say something like, "I'd scream," "I'd stay very quiet and try to find a way out," or, "I'd close my eyes and pray hard!" Some have suggested joining "Team Jacob" or "Team Edward." A better answer might be, *quit pretending*.

My clients are surprised how quickly they forgot I said *pretend* you are in a cave. Instead, they immediately pictured themselves in a literal dark cave with monsters, and imagined what they would do if they were actually there. I use this riddle to illustrate how quickly we can lock ourselves into a model or paradigm of thinking, and how we will craft responses and behaviors to deal with our supposed reality.

Each one of us has a unique belief system about the world. We see it through the lens of our own self-concept, which colors our perceptions. We create a personal version of reality composed primarily of our notions, opinions, and subjective conclusions, filtered through how we feel about ourselves. We generally proceed as if our beliefs and our perspectives were a complete certainty. We behave as if our paradigm were an absolute reality. But is it? And does it matter?

Yes, it does matter—greatly. If our belief paradigm is based on reasonably rational thoughts, beliefs, and feelings, which can be modified positively by additional life experience, we can be fairly healthy and functional people. However, if our paradigm is irrational and not amenable to new information, it is delusional; and will leave us susceptible to addiction, or unable to break-free once addicted. A vital part of treatment is identification of the irrational core beliefs that are keeping an addict trapped in his cyclical pattern.

Core Beliefs

Any belief system is composed of a combination of values, attitudes, and ideas incorporated from life experiences. Myths are also incorporated. Beliefs include things we have learned from peers, family, and culture, and ideas and conclusions we have drawn on our own. We have formed beliefs about sex, relationships, and the roles of men and women. Naturally, most of our beliefs, such as the belief about our own inherent worth, or whether others are trustworthy and dependable, derive from life experience. Beliefs about relationships are especially dependent upon experience. Our belief system influences our expectations, shapes our perceptions, and in many ways determines our behaviors and responses.

An example of a healthy, positive belief about one's self is, "I'm a likeable person and people enjoy being with me." A healthy belief about others is, "There are many kind and helpful people in the world." These beliefs are adaptive and useful. Certain behaviors and expectations would follow, such as, "I can be involved with others and let them get to know me, and get to know them, and expect positive responses most of the time."

Conversely, addicts have *negative core beliefs*, which are like monsters that prey upon their minds. Because they are in a dark cave mentally, impaired thinking results and manifests in an addict's mechanisms of denial—maladaptive, self-deceptive responses used to cope with their false beliefs. Poor decisions are made, harmful actions are taken, and the pattern repeats. The *addictive system* is therefore, a construct of an addict's own fractured thinking. It begins with one's negative core beliefs.

Negative Core Beliefs

Unfortunately, for sex addicts, negative core beliefs are an element of the storm that dominates their thinking and drives their behavior. An addict has four primary negative core beliefs—irrational beliefs—

that interfere with healthy functioning:

- "I am a flawed and unworthy person."

- "If people knew me, they would not love me."

- "My needs will never be met if I have to count on others."

- "Sex is my most important need."[33]

"I am a flawed and unworthy person," is a reflection of self-image, which leads to social isolation and guardedness.

"If people knew me, they wouldn't love me," is a belief about relationships, which leads to the creation of a manipulative pseudo-self to please others, win acceptance, or gain power and control.

"My needs will never be met if I have to count on others," leads to mistrust and expectations of disappointment.

"Sex is my most important need," is a view of sexuality that leads to the manipulation of sex as a substitute for intimacy. It is in this belief that sex addicts differ from those with other addictions. Others believe their own addictions—drugs, alcohol, gambling—is their most important need.

Mechanisms of Denial

Addicts also develop mechanisms of denial—self-deceptions—to cope with their negative core beliefs and their addictions. These denial mechanisms are excuses that deflect responsibility for an addict's beliefs and behaviors, and allow avoidance of accountability for the addiction's consequences. The mechanisms/deceptions include:

- *Denial*—suppression of conscious awareness that helps an addict avoid the reality of his addiction and its consequences

- *Rationalization*—justifying or explaining-away

unacceptable behavior

- *Minimizing*—excusing behaviors or consequences as less significant than they are

- *Blaming*—pointing to other persons or events as causing the problem

- *Compartmentalizing*—segregating thinking and feelings about an addiction from conflicting thoughts, values, beliefs, and actions

- *All-or-nothing thinking*—insisting that something or someone is completely one way or another

- *Distortions*—misinterpreting others' intentions as more positive or negative than they are

These mechanisms of denial interfere with the ability of an addict to absorb helpful new information and to properly examine or modify his belief system. They prevent an addict from being self-accountable for his behavior. Everyone uses self-deception occasionally to avoid painful or difficult realizations; however, addicts' denial mechanisms dominate their thinking, which blocks the insight necessary to break their system of addiction.

A severe symptom of addiction is the denial mechanism of blaming—the belief that it is *always* someone else's fault. "I have never had any breaks, so I deserve whatever I can get." Or, "If my wife would just be more fun in bed, it wouldn't be such an issue." Others are blamed as the cause for the behaviors and consequences of an addiction. Distancing from responsibility demonstrates a lack of personal ownership for an addict's problems. This is immature thinking. Such blaming is a normal characteristic of young children, but in addicts it is a good barometer of the severity of the addiction, and the level of recovery challenge that lies ahead.

Life Stress and Chaotic Living

The storm gathers strength as the delusional thinking of an addict inevitably creates stress and chaos across multiple sectors of his life: Relationships suffer; self-care is usually neglected; work performance can deteriorate; finances may be poorly managed; disconnection from typical interests and social life often occurs; and normal life stressors feel exaggerated as the addict struggles to stay afloat in the turmoil. An addict's life stress lends to further impairment of his thinking and diminishes his ability to make thoughtful choices and consider potential consequences. The desire to escape into the addiction intensifies.

Acting-Out Cycle

Overwhelmed by negative core beliefs, mechanisms of denial, stress and chaotic living, an addict will surrender to the acting-out cycle of his addiction to escape. The acting-out cycle consists of:

- *Preoccupation*—mentally rehearsing, planning, and anticipating the addictive behaviors

- *Ritualizing*—engaging in a series of behaviors prior to acting-out that have become arousing by association

- *Compulsivity*—losing the ability to choose whether or not to engage in a behavior

- *Despair*—experiencing a profound feeling of hopelessness[34]

The despair that an addict experiences after an acting-out cycle confirms the inner-voice that declares, "I am a bad person," "Nobody could love me," "I cannot depend on anyone else," and, "Sex is my most important need." Again, his mechanisms of denial engage, and in turn this delusional thinking fuels yet another acting-out cycle. The intensity of the preoccupation, ritualization, and compulsivity increases, and the shame and despair builds with each cycle. The addiction deepens, the storm darkens, and the danger escalates.

Breaking Up the Storm

A sex addict is in a dark cave flooded by his own negative core beliefs and self-deceptions. No amount of evasive or combative tactics will save him from the monsters. Neither screaming, nor hiding will get him out of the cave. This is because the cave and the monsters do not really exist. Negative core beliefs and the accompanying ineffective denial responses trap the addict in a world of unreality.

An addict's addictive behaviors are symptoms of an underlying illness—a dysfunctional belief and denial system. His negative belief system requires healing. His long-engrained mindset must be changed. This is difficult because his distorted perspective seems entirely real to him. It is a necessary component of an addict's recovery to understand that he has, and how he came to have, such negative core beliefs. This provides a foundational context for understanding one's self. Breaking down the mechanisms of denial leads to better self-awareness and accountability, so that the negative core beliefs can be altered. Ultimately, an addict's confidence and self-worth must be repaired, and the belief that sex is his most important need must be surrendered.

Primarily targeting the addictive behaviors will fail as a strategy of recovery. The aim should not be to get a sex addict to stop visiting prostitutes or online porn sites, or having serial affairs or risky sex at roadside parks, merely because those things are "bad." Such attempts are like my clients' responses to the riddle—the wrong level of solution. An addict may be able to cease his addictive behaviors temporarily, but real recovery occurs when one is freed from the dark cave of distorted beliefs and self-deceptions. This freedom is a precursor to removing the overwhelming desire to escape by acting-out with sex.

Recovery is a paradigm shift to a new set of beliefs, values, and attitudes from which healthy behavior can emerge. An addict must come to believe, "I am a good person," "Others can love me and find me worthwhile," "I can trust others and treat them in a manner that they can trust me," and, "I have many needs in relationships." The addict must learn to stop blaming, denying, minimizing, and relying on other self-deceptions. If an addict progresses beyond negative beliefs and denial, eventually the urges to act-out will be minimized, and the addict will find that real relationships can be nurturing and fulfilling. Fantasy will not seem so seductive. This shift, however, requires a sustained and dedicated effort.

.

CHAPTER NINE

The Storm of Companion Addictions

'Round and 'round it goes,
Where it stops, nobody knows... [35]

Carnival Barker

The devastation of a major storm results from a combination of horrendous winds, torrential rain, and flooding in densely populated areas. Likewise, the consequences of the storm of sex addiction are worse when multiple addictions combine. Additional addictions add intensity and increase the risk of personal destruction. The interplay and compounding of multiple addictions and the resulting symptom intensification is called *Addiction Interaction Disorder* (AID).[36]

It is essential for a sex addict, his family, and his therapist to understand AID if sex addiction treatment is to be successful. A primary cause of relapse is overlooking companion addictions in an addict's *cluster* of addictions, and therefore, failing to monitor and treat them, too. Repeated relapses and switching between alternative addictions is characteristic of AID. Managing multiple addictions can be a confusing game of Whac-A-Mole. Everyone needs to see the big picture in recovery, and progress needs to be evaluated with some level of scrutiny by all parties.

There is rarely only one addiction at play, especially with sex addiction. Several addictions may not only co-exist, but also interact, reinforce, intensify, and replace one another.[37] Because they influence the probability of successful treatment outcomes, it is imperative that a therapist and an addict identify any companion addictions and monitor them throughout recovery, even if they have been dormant for some time. To accomplish this it is necessary to have some knowledge of the variety of addiction interactions that may occur.

Four Categories of Addiction and Addictive Behavior

The compulsions most frequently associated with the word addiction are those involving substance abuse, such as alcoholism; or behavioral problems, such as addiction to gambling or sex. People may also be familiar with relationship-type addictions such as codependency. But many people are surprised to learn that incessant retreat into negative core affect states—despair, shame, rage, resentment, and self-loathing—can reinforce or replace a primary addiction. Some addicts camp out in this inner-cranial bar, by habitually indulging in irrational thoughts and exaggerated feelings.

An addict's cluster may include addictions or compulsions in one or more of four main categories:

- *Substances*—alcohol, cocaine, nicotine, methamphetamine, marijuana, medication

- *Processes*—sex, gambling, gaming, eating, exercising, working, spending

- *Compulsive relating*—codependency, love addiction/love avoidance, romance, trauma bonding

- *Core affect states*—shame, misery, despair, self-loathing, rage[38]

An addict may combine elements in any of the four categories to create his own unique profile of addiction—his "designer drug." For example, a common cluster of addictions observed in sex addicts, is combining compulsive sexual behavior with gambling and alcohol abuse. The loss of control that characterizes addiction may occur across all categories, or only in one or two. An important point to remember is that there is probably another addiction or two lurking in the shadows, ready to step up and fill the gap for an addict who is experiencing cravings while abstaining from his primary addiction.

In addition to co-occurring addictions, an addict may also have periods of intentional starvation from his primary addiction—that are actually part of his particular addiction cycle. If a sex addict in recovery is not presently exhibiting addictive behaviors, it may be that he is truly gaining sobriety, or it may be an indication of temporary compulsive avoidance of sexual thoughts and behaviors.

It is a sex addict's need to get *any* kind of fix, which must be treated. This is not accomplished merely by gaining abstinence from the primary addiction. A sex addict who is abstinent, and therefore appears to be in early recovery, may simply have switched to an avoidant side of the addiction, or to another addiction in his cluster.

Obtaining a psycho-sexual history and constructing a timeline of significant life events can help identify companion addictions to be monitored. Compiling a multi-generational family genogram may reveal addictions in a family system to which an addict is susceptible. The history, timeline, and the family genogram provide much needed information about an individual's AID pattern, and help the addict understand sex addiction as a brain disorder and a chronic illness.

Addiction Interactions

The dynamic interaction of addictions is illustrated in the diagram, *The Storm of Companion Addictions*. It can be used as a guide for screening and monitoring for potential companion addictions.

The Storm of
Companion Addictions

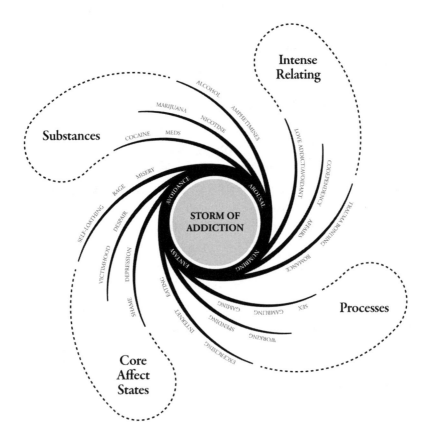

Let us look at some of the recognizable patterns that sex addicts may exhibit:

Cross tolerance describes the simultaneous increase in two or more addictions. For example, a sex addiction and gambling addiction become worse at the same time. Cross tolerance also refers to the abrupt transfer of a high level of activity from one addiction to another. In Kate's case, her computer crashed and she could no longer spend hours every night using social media and having online romances. Her level of tolerance for mood-altering online behavior transferred to alcohol, and within weeks she was regularly binging on beer.

Withdrawal mediation is an addict's use of one addiction to ease the discomfort of withdrawal from another. An alcoholic's abuse of caffeine, nicotine, or sugar to mediate withdrawal from alcohol is a common example. A sex addict who gets married might mediate withdrawal from serial affair behavior by gambling online, or by reverting to excessive drinking.

Replacement occurs when one addiction replaces another with similar behavioral features and emotional effects. For example, when Stanley retired from his powerful position as a CEO, within a year he was frequenting strip bars, partying, and having risky sex. He replaced the euphoria of his compulsive working and high-stakes financial transactions, with "rescuing" young women from financial and relationship crises.

Alternating describes cycles of switching between addictions, or between behaviors within an addiction, in a predictable pattern. Dean's periods of having affairs with married women alternated with months of drinking and binging on pornography at home.

Masking occurs when an addict uses one addiction to cover for another that may pose a more serious risk or is less socially acceptable. Mark used his compulsive drinking to hide his seductive role sex addiction from his wife. He minimized his flirtatious behavior toward his wife's friends at social gatherings by blaming it on having "one too many." Also, "Meeting some of the guys at the bar after work," provided his cover for cruising for women. Sex addicts often mask their sex addiction because they feel shame or fear severe consequences.

Ritualizing is using a series of behaviors to induce a trance-like state prior to acting-out. Rituals are part of the addiction, and an addict may derive more pleasure from the rituals than the sexual behavior itself. Jerry's rituals often began in the morning when he looked at pornography and imagined the encounter he hoped to have that evening. He continued to have sexual fantasies throughout the day. After work, he felt sexually aroused as he changed his clothes, applied fresh cologne, and brushed his hair before setting out to cruise several parks. He parked his car and pretended to read a book. The risk of getting spotted by someone he knew, or even arrested, increased the excitement and arousal as the scenario progressed. If he was "lucky," a stranger invited him to the public restroom where they had sex. The encounters were over quickly, but his fantasy and rituals sustained Jerry's arousal for hours.

Combining is using two or more addictions together for the purpose of generating a more potent effect; for example, using cocaine and sex. Combining for intensity may involve the use of multiple addictions simultaneously, in an overlapping series, or in a serial fashion. Binges can last hours or days.

Numbing is a pattern of engaging in high-arousal behaviors, followed by behaviors or use of substances that soothe or sedate. Beth, for example, often followed her online cruising and clandestine hook-ups with strangers, with compulsive eating and drinking.

Disinhibiting occurs when one addiction lowers inhibitions for acting-out in another. Bill drank alcohol before his clandestine dates, which reduced feelings of self-consciousness about his appearance, and blunted his judgment about the risks of having sexual rendezvous with married women.[39]

Avoidance

Compulsive avoidance behaviors—the flipside of excessive behaviors—can also be an integral part of AID. A classic example is the compulsive overeater who becomes food avoidant, thus alternating between periods of overeating and extreme dieting. A sex addict can also switch to the avoidant side of his addiction and alternate between sexual excess and compulsive sexual avoidance. Avoidance can be misinterpreted as healthy progress by an unsuspecting therapist who mistakes it for abstinence.

An addict can be preoccupied by *aversion* to sexual contact, and compulsively avoid situations in which sexual feelings, thoughts, or opportunities might arise. Avoidance is a defense against feelings of fear, shame, and loss of control related to intimacy, dependency, and desire. By avoiding, an addict feels in control by fighting addictive urges internally, rather than controlling emotions by acting-out. The addict is basically thinking, "I can take care of myself. I don't have to depend on others to meet my needs," which provides feelings of safety, superiority, and power. Some addicts may be avoidant with a significant other (with whom they fear emotional vulnerability), but remain compulsively sexual with pornography, prostitutes, or affair partners.

Sexual avoidance may be part of an addict's cluster, and should be assessed along with acting-out behaviors.

Lindsay and the Complexity of Companion Addictions

Lindsay came to see me because she had been having panic attacks and insomnia since her husband, John, had suggested a trial separation and told her that he was considering a career opportunity in another city. She was furious at John for planning to "abandon" her and was terrified at the thought of being alone.

John joined Lindsay for her next session so that I could learn more about his concerns about their marriage. I asked if he would share with me why he was thinking about a separation.

John said quietly, "Well, like I have tried to tell Lindsay, I feel that I can't do anything right in her eyes, and besides, she is so busy with her work and activities that she has no time or energy for our relationship."

"You sound pretty discouraged." I said.

John nodded, glanced at Lindsay, and then replied, "Yes, and worried. I have been really concerned about how much she is drinking, too. But when I try to talk to her she says, 'I don't want to talk about this right now,' or something like that."

Lindsay was defensive. "John is exaggerating. Things aren't that bad. After all, I am busy. I have a really stressful job and a teenager. I like to have a drink with my friends once in a while to relax," she said, a bit sarcastically.

At her next session, Lindsay admitted, "I don't know why I feel so annoyed with John all the time. He just gets on my nerves." She confided that she wondered if she had made a mistake by marrying him, because he seemed "boring" and "not very ambitious."

As I gradually came to know Lindsay better, I discovered that she learned early in life to be on guard in relationships, and to expect people to leave her. As a child she witnessed her parents' frightening fights and multiple separations.

Lindsay's sexual acting-out and alcohol abuse began in adolescence and escalated in college. Eventually, she was charged with a third DUI and sentenced to community-based outpatient treatment. After that, she was cautious about drinking, but not about men. She had several abusive live-in boyfriends, one of whom nearly killed her in a physical assault when he discovered she was hooking-up on dating sites for sex. A police officer called to the scene after that event asked Lindsay out on a date a few weeks later. He made Lindsay feel special and safe and they were soon married. Lindsay described their marriage as a "disaster," and blamed their problems on her husband's job and night shifts. Lindsay continued to hook-up with guys online and excused her affairs and romances by saying, "I just couldn't stand being alone all the time."

After her divorce from the cop, Lindsay was wary of relationships, but she continued to cruise online. When she met John, he seemed like a perfect match. John was handsome and successful in his business. He was loving and considerate to her and her daughter, and his friends reassured her that he was a "great guy." Lindsay thought, "All of my troubles are behind me." But not long after they were married, Lindsay began to drink again. It increased to several glasses of wine in the evening, and binging when she went out with friends on the weekends. Although she had tried to stop, she resumed hooking-up online but managed to hide it with elaborate cover-ups. Behind her facade of defensiveness, she felt ashamed and lived in fear of being discovered.

Lindsay had switched between, or combined her addictions, in various ways over time. Sex addiction, work addiction, and drinking were currently providing mood-altering arousal and numbing to escape from her loneliness and shame. Love avoidance helped her manage her fear of vulnerability and feelings of inadequacy in her marriage. But her addictions were creating severe consequences and depriving her of what she wanted most—a caring relationship.

In therapy, Lindsay learned that she was re-enacting the painful losses of her childhood; she was unconsciously setting herself up to feel buried fear and rage, and to be "abandoned" again. Lindsay began taking an antidepressant, and with the support of her husband and family, she persisted in her treatment and recovery. She slowly learned to live in the present without shame and fear, and to feel the comfort of safe relationships.

Monitoring for Companion Addictions

Just like the destructive potential of a tropical storm is the result of a combination of intensifying forces, the storm of companion addictions is created by an addict's unique combination of multiple addictions, and can also escalate and spiral out of control. AID has hurricane-like potential to unleash its fury and cut a wide path of personal and relationship destruction. Effective response to sex addiction requires a thorough assessment that correctly identifies the scope and direction of the storm, tracks its prior movements, and prepares an addict and his family with adequate knowledge and safeguards to deal with the impact until the storm has passed. Having awareness of the chaotic nature of the storm of sex addiction, along with a detailed treatment response plan, which includes monitoring for companion addictions, will help addicts and their families withstand the storm and rebuild their lives.

PART THREE

SURVIVING THE STORM

CHAPTER TEN

THE PATH OF RECOVERY

A Hero's Journey

*Where there had been only fearful emptiness... there is now unfolding
an unexpected wealth of vitality. It is not a homecoming since this home
had never before existed. It is the discovery of home.*[40]

Alice Miller

We are born with a longing for right relationship
with ourselves and others, and the innate capacity
to recognize such relationships. This desire and
intuition is the source of energy for an addict's
travels on the road to wellbeing, a path upon which a hero's journey of
transformation may unfold.

Heroes, whether Odysseus, Luke Skywalker, Harry Potter, Dorothy
from Kansas—or a recovering addict—are often thrust apprehensively
into their transformational journeys. They struggle to overcome dark
forces within and without, and are assisted along the way by helpers.
Through self-reflection and perseverance, heroes emerge strengthened
as they grow more conscious of their true selves, higher values, and
social responsibilities.

Many men and women have made the hero's journey of recovery

from sex addiction. In this chapter we will discuss how the experiences of recovering addicts, a body of clinical evidence, and new brain research provide knowledge that is being used to assist addicts in their journeys to regaining healthy lives. We will begin by reviewing the warning signs that can alert an addict, his family, or a treatment provider to a sex addiction problem, and how an addict's pathological denial can impede his recognizing these signs. We will discuss the stages of recovery—pre-recovery, when a problem is first assessed; early recovery, in which an addict gains abstinence and becomes accountable for his problems; and stable recovery, in which an addict is dedicated to his sober thinking and wellness.

I will present the Five Factor Wellness Model, the framework for my outpatient treatment process at STARPRO (Sexual Treatment and Recovery Program) in Omaha, Nebraska. The Five Factor Wellness Model is an example of modern treatment approaches that help an addict access his or her own innate healing potential, and build a strong foundation for stable recovery.

Warning Signs

The warning signs that problematic sexual behavior may have progressed to addiction, and that further assessment is needed, include the following:

- Struggling to control sexual thoughts and behaviors

- Losing or impairing relationships because of the inability to stop sexual activities outside a primary relationship

- Lying about unaccounted for time that involved sexual activities

- Feeling guilty or shameful after engaging in sexual thoughts, fantasies, or behaviors

- Routinely pursuing sexual activities online

- Resorting to sex to escape, relieve anxiety, or cope with problems

- Losing time from work pursuing sexual activities

- Engaging in criminal sexual behaviors such as soliciting prostitutes, sexual harassment, or child pornography

- Participating in sexual activities that violate one's own values

- Blaming others for one's sexual behaviors

- Putting self at risk for STDs

Even when they exhibit multiple warning signs similar to those above, addicts generally do not recognize that their problems are rooted in addiction because they are trapped in their dark caves—their delusional states of denial. Dean was in deep denial when his family urged him to see me. He had lost two jobs, his insurance and retirement benefits, and was facing charges because of intense sexual scenarios. He had a long history of online pornography use and hook-ups, and regularly had affairs with married women. My assessment confirmed that he had a serious problem with sex addiction. I was not surprised when Dean disagreed and gave me his own distorted perspective: "I don't think I really have an addiction. It is just that my girlfriend lies to me all the time. She just makes me crazy."

Stages of Recovery

Severe consequences or a crisis precipitated by addictive behavior may be a wake-up call that begins to weaken the denial system of addicts like Dean. Perhaps desperate lies about cybersex or affairs can no longer prevent the collapse of an addict's marriage, or his sordid sexual secrets are made public. Perhaps exhaustion and shame are too much to bear and the addict becomes severely depressed or suicidal. An addict in this pre-recovery stage may seek help, yet cling to denial. He often blames others for his behavior, or tells his wife or therapist some version of, "I know I can stop, if I really want to." He may attempt to "white-knuckle" it through a period of abstinence to prove he can quit, but solo or cynical efforts are doomed to fail and relapse is inevitable.

In the early recovery stage, which may last one or two years or more, a sex addict gains abstinence from acting-out behaviors, usually with the support of others. He begins to see reality more clearly, and to realize that his mood-altering sexual behaviors are symptoms of addictive thinking that have affected important aspects of his life. As my client Jim declared, "I can accept the fact that I can never use porn or drink again. What is more difficult to accept is that all of my problems are of my own making!" With this statement, Jim was becoming accountable for the lonely life he had created, and the consequences he was experiencing.

For his recovery to proceed in earnest, an addict must face the truth—that he is out of control and powerless over the addiction—and that he needs the help of others to gain sobriety. Accepting his need for support is a crucial move. The necessary transformation of core beliefs and distorted perspectives that maintain the addictive behavior can only be accomplished in concert with others who support recovery.

STARPRO—The Five Factor Wellness Model

When an addict is willing to accept help, a trained addiction therapist can collaborate with him to design a treatment plan that will reduce his risk of relapse and lead to stable recovery. At STARPRO and other treatment programs, the process begins with a comprehensive assessment of the addict's life circumstances and history, to determine if a problem involving sex, is actually a sex *addiction* problem. If an addiction problem exists, the addict's particular types of sex and other companion addictions will be evaluated, and an initial opinion will be given regarding the severity of the problem and its potential causation. A treatment approach is then recommended. The standardized industry tools for assessment of sex addiction are the Sexual Addiction Screening Test, the Sex Addiction Assessment, and the Sexual Dependency Inventory.[41]

Besides screening for sex addiction, it is important to identify other compulsive behaviors and addictions, as well as any accompanying physical and mental health issues. Additional testing may be advisable if the assessment indicates it would be useful. A careful evaluation of each addict's unique addiction story and family system history is essential for designing a successful treatment plan.

Competent mental health professionals and addiction specialists who can provide initial assessments and make treatment recommendations are available in many communities. Certified Sex Addiction Therapists, who are specifically trained in sex addiction assessment and treatment, can be located by geographic area at www.iitap.net. Inpatient treatment facilities and specialized outpatient programs are available around the country if a higher level of care is needed or desired.

The STARPRO Five Factor Wellness Model provides an addict and his family a reliable framework for the journey of recovery. It incorporates what research has shown to be vital to healing the addict's hijacked brain—effectively addressing denial responses, trauma experience, regulation of emotions, maladaptive coping mechanisms, and intimacy skills—in an all-out effort to build sustained recovery. Let us take a look at each of the components of the STARPRO Model— Recovery First, Self-Care, Therapy, Support Group, and Meditation:

Factor One: Recovery First

In the Star Wars saga, Yoda the Jedi Master, reproves Luke Skywalker's half-hearted effort at levitating his star-cruiser from the Degobah swamp. "Do or do not," Yoda scolds. "There is no try." Likewise, a mediocre attempt at recovery will not succeed, because the powerful dark lord of addiction is waiting in the shadows for an opportunity to attack and seize control. By making a whole-hearted commitment to recovery above all else, an addict who was previously willing to risk everything for a fix, can succeed in regaining his sanity, and possibly save his marriage, kids, and career. Some addicts even save their own lives.

M. Scott Peck, author of *A Road Less Traveled*, describes this all-out effort as a "dedication to reality at all costs."[42] This means recovery activities are prioritized and other responsibilities and events are scheduled around them. An addict may decide to sacrifice a job or end a relationship to remove himself from an environment that invites relapse. With the guidance of his therapist or sponsor, the addict can judiciously disclose his problem to significant others and family to enlist their involvement. The self-shaming addict is often surprised by the support he receives from friends, family, and other associates when he begins recovery. His "dedication to reality at all costs" may require admitting himself to inpatient treatment if he is unable to gain stable recovery otherwise. The addict who builds a strong recovery does not merely "try." He does whatever it takes to get well.

Factor Two: Individual and Group Therapy

To effectively address the underlying issues of shame, loneliness, and fear of intimacy that drive the addiction and increase the risk of relapse, individual therapy is essential. Therapy is an opportunity for an addict to experience a mutual relationship in which his needs and feelings can be felt and expressed safely. A caring and non-reactive therapist provides a secure base from which a client can explore internal conflicts, learn to manage strong emotions, and try new ways of thinking and operating in the world.

As an addict progresses in therapy and remembers more painful memories previously repressed, he grieves what was lost in childhood, but also reclaims memories of positive experiences as well. He may recall an important person in his life, a "helping witness," who cared about and connected with him. As the addict in recovery realizes what he overcame in early life, he eventually sees himself more compassionately, feels more worthy, and forgives those who harmed him. Rather than feeling, "I was a bad child, unworthy of care," he comes to feel, "I went through a bad time and found a way to survive."

In addition to individual therapy, group therapy in a sexual sobriety group is a cornerstone of treatment at STARPRO. Group therapy offers the opportunity to practice accountability to self and others. Being reliable, listening to others without judging, and sharing thoughts and feelings are relationship skills that may not have been acquired in an addict's early life experience, and cannot be learned in isolation or though social media. *Facing the Shadow*, a workbook by Patrick Carnes, is utilized in the sexual sobriety group at STARPRO.[43] It outlines a progressive series of tasks necessary for recovery and provides important information about addiction. Psycho-education about relevant concepts is an important aspect of the program at STARPRO, and is woven into the treatment process.

For example, addicts learn about the brain functioning involved in craving, which an addict experiences as an intense wave of desire. "One minute I was fine and the next minute I was sitting in front of the computer looking at porn again," is an implausible explanation unless one understands that craving can bypass rational thinking. Addicts also learn about stress response syndrome, an addict's reflex-like response to stressful stimuli—a mental state in which cognition tends to shut down and out-of-proportion emotions take over. Addicts learn about the concept of neural plasticity, which confirms that it is possible to retrain the brain to identify and avoid triggers, and to build new neuropathways that allow more conscious choices and more positive adaptive responses. They learn how trauma resolution and stress management may help them modulate exaggerated emotional responses.

Through the course of therapy, addicts ultimately learn that they have acquired layers of unhealthy coping behaviors, some of which were a child's only means of surviving trauma when he did not have the nurturance and protection he needed. These coping mechanisms, such as negative core beliefs, protective fantasy, and avoidance of intimacy, must be addressed to resolve addiction and to reduce the risk of relapse.

For an addict in recovery, using new knowledge and insight gained in therapy contributes to less shameful thinking, more understanding of his own emotions, more rational responses to stressful situations, better relationship skills, and less acting-out with sex.

Factor Three: Support Group

Addicts who actively participate in support groups and work the steps with a sponsor who has his or her own stable recovery, have a much better chance of sustained recovery themselves. Sexaholics Anonymous, Sex Addicts Anonymous, Sex and Love Addicts Anonymous, and S-Anon (for partners) have chapters throughout the country. Celebrate Recovery groups are offered in many faith communities. All of these groups are modeled similarly to Alcoholics Anonymous. Many cities also have 16 Steps for Discovery and Empowerment groups based on a model developed by Charlotte Kasl, author of *Many Roads, One Journey: Moving Beyond the 12 Steps.*[44]

An active step-based program is the "weight room" where an addict exercises the radical beliefs and behaviors of a well person. Working through a program with a sponsor is a soul-searching process of self-reflection, and an amends-making process to those he or she has harmed, which helps the addict become a more accountable person and keep the day-by-day "dedication to reality at all costs."

Factor Four: Self-Care

The Fourth Factor in the STARPRO Wellness Model is basic self-care—a healthy lifestyle that includes good nutrition; regular exercise; a sleep routine; stress management; pleasant social interaction; time with family and friends; and healthy emotional and physical boundaries. An addict learns to tune in to the messages from his body about basic needs that he had been ignoring, to monitor self-care regularly, and to establish healthier practices. Most recovering addicts will agree that these basic dependency needs are important for overall wellbeing, but they often seriously neglect their own self-care. Self-neglect is evidence that an addict does not feel worthy of his own effort or attention, much less deserve the care of others.

Self-nurturing helps an addict feel more worthy of love and respect from himself and others. When he esteems himself by tending to his own basic needs, he becomes more prepared for healthy relationships because he is not looking for someone to "parent" him. Basic self-care is essential for valuing one's self, which is a prerequisite for valuing other people and building mutually caring relationships.

Factor Five: Meditation and Mindfulness

Activities such as meditation, meditative journaling, prayer, deep relaxation, yoga, tai chi, painting, drawing, and listening to music, are powerful tools for recovery. When addicts incorporate regular meditation or other mindfulness practices into their daily routines, they progress more quickly and have stronger recoveries. Meditation may be as beneficial as antidepressant medication to support mood and reduce anxiety. Meditation improves an addict's ability to calm, center, and be more reflective about his emotions and experiences.

> *Jeff, one of my sex addiction clients who incorporated daily meditation into his recovery program, found that he began to respond to parenting situations with his child more calmly. In the past when his son had disappointments, such as not making the varsity basketball team, Jeff thought, "I'm a failure as a father," and experienced feelings of shame and anger, followed by cravings to escape into sexual fantasy. Nowadays, Jeff can be present and sympathetic to his son's feelings, rather than absorbed in his own. He can say to himself, "My son really wanted to be on the varsity team, but there will be other opportunities for him."*

Following the Five Factor Wellness Model

By following the Five Factor Wellness Model, which integrates the necessary components of recovery, an addict practices new thought patterns and behaviors that are more beneficial responses to his emotions and life challenges. Rather than using addictive behaviors or coping mechanisms he learned in early life, he has healthy alternatives—positive self-soothing, expressing feelings and emotions appropriately, responding to situations constructively, and connecting to others for support.

The recovery process at STARPRO also helps addicts identify the strengths they bring to the healing process—their own wisdom, life experience, and accomplishments. After all, many of them are remarkably resilient people. They have survived difficult childhoods, may have obtained educations, or functioned well in their businesses or jobs. Many have developed their talents, contributed to their professions, and held leadership roles in their communities. Although they may have struggled in intimate relationships or in being emotionally present to their own children, they may also have provided for their families and conveyed positive values as well.

Whether an addict's problem is based in childhood trauma or self-induced trauma from iPorn, the sex addict who makes a commitment to recovery can begin to understand and overcome his illness, and to revalue his personhood. Ultimately, with the help of others and the rigorous practice of the components of recovery, he will replace addictions with more adaptive ways of coping, forgive himself, and reclaim his life and his dignity.

By following his innate longing for right relationship, and by having the courage to embark upon a hero's journey of recovery, the sex addict discovers that the peace he was seeking is within. He replaces shame with compassion, isolation with connection, and he reclaims his capacity for authentic relationship with himself and others. His sustained "dedication to reality at all costs" brings him back to true self, and perhaps for the first time in a very long time, or even for the first time in his life, he may feel, "I am finally home."

CHAPTER ELEVEN

EXCAVATING THE AUTHENTIC SELF

Is Anybody In There?

We make ourselves a place apart
Behind light words that tease and flout,
But oh, the agitated heart
Till someone find us really out

'Tis pity if the case require
(Or so we say) that in the end
We speak the literal to inspire
The understanding of a friend

But so with all, from babes that play
At hide-and-seek to God afar
So all who hide too well away
Must speak and tell us where they are.[45]

Revelation by Robert Frost

"Something was missing in my life," Sharon whispered as she choked back her tears. "My husband and I started swinging and hooking-up online and other stuff, but now we're fighting a lot and I feel more alone than ever." Sharon is a natural beauty who has a promising career, but she is severely depressed and has put her job in jeopardy with too many absences from work. Sharon described how her husband, Rick, has encouraged her affairs, including a current affair with Mike, a married man they met at a party. "I'm with Mike one day, then Rick the next. Yeah, the sex is fun, but I'm so jealous and scared all the time because I know they have sex with other girls, too." Sharon shuttered and exclaimed, "It makes me so crazy. I just want to be special to someone!"

Sharon's relationships have the drama and unpredictability of a soap opera, but lack the fulfilling intimacy for which she longs. Why does Sharon endure this miserable situation? Why has living on the edge of uncertainty become so compelling for her?

Sharon's insecurities can be traced to her early life. As far back as she can recall, her parents were consumed with their own problems, and too busy, exhausted, or neglectful to notice her needs, wants, or feelings. Sharon's earliest memories are of the afterschool ritual at her house. When she arrived home and walked into the living room, her father, a drunk, jobless, television junkie, would greet her with, "Get me a sandwich." She would assemble the sandwich, serve it to her father, and sit by him on the couch in silence. She rarely got a glance from him, and never got a hug. She knew from experience that if she interrupted his television viewing he would get very angry.

Throughout her childhood, Sharon felt disconnected and lonely, and coped by trying to be quiet and helpful. She longed for her parents to touch her or talk to her, but they scarcely talked to each other—only screamed—and there was no interaction with extended family. By age fourteen her model for relationships—needing people who were not there for her emotionally—was firmly established. She would thereafter mistake intensity for caring.

Jerry, a thirty-six-year-old gay man, is also longing for closeness but hooked on intensity. He is a local celebrity, known for his talented acting and singing in theater productions. In his first session with me Jerry said, "What I really want is a committed relationship with a life partner." However, Jerry has been acting-out in high-risk anonymous sex for years, and is unable to stop. If he is arrested, he could lose his job, his children, and the respect of the community.

"Jerry, what do you think makes you take such chances?" I asked.

He thought for a minute then replied, "I guess it makes me feel desired and special, and I want that."

"But you would probably have sex with pretty much any man who shows up, right?" I asked. Jerry nodded. "And, wouldn't the other guy have sex with anyone who shows up, too?" He nodded again. "That doesn't make you very special does it? That just makes you the guy who showed up."

Jerry pondered the point as if he had never thought of it that way before, and though a little defensive in tone, conceded, "I guess you are right."

What I was doing with Jerry was "spitting in the soup," a technique to interrupt irrational thinking. My frank remark helped Jerry notice that his behavior is inconsistent with what he really wants for himself. Habitual anonymous sex does not lead to being cherished. But why has Jerry failed to see that his behaviors are counterproductive to finding the committed relationship he really wants? Why does he continue to take such risks?

Sadly, both Sharon and Jerry are sex addicts who are not only hooked on sexual intensity, but also on the strong emotions of fear, anger, and jealousy. Both are repeating the emotional abandonment they experienced in childhood, complete with the fruitless longing to be "special."

Sex addicts are trapped in painful and dangerous relationships for reasons that are largely unconscious to them. They long for connection but use sexual behavior and relationship intensity like a drug, and choreograph situations in which real intimacy is impossible. They find others who enable their compulsions.

Indeed, "something is missing" for Sharon and Jerry, but it is not the lovers they "crave" in a transient state of panic or loneliness. It is the authentic self—their ability to be directly aware of their inner needs and feelings—and to use this internal gyroscope of self-awareness for navigating the world of relationships.

False Selves

Cut adrift from an anchoring sense of authentic self and awash in the turbulence of child-like emotions, addicts often slip into protective, false-self states they developed earlier in life. Below the surface Sharon feels like a terrified child whose mother has disappeared. She finds occasional solitude and loneliness to be unbearable, rather than a normal part of life. She fears abandonment when she is with a partner, and feels abandoned when she is not. She grasps for attention and compulsively calls and texts her husband, lovers, or friends for relief. She ruminates about her partners cheating on her, or indulges in euphoric fantasies about her next romantic reunion. Her panic and neediness push people away and lead to unstable relationships.

Sharon may also switch into an adaptive, "good girl" self, one who learned to sacrifice to please and accommodate her parents in an attempt to prevent disconnection. This illusion of control calmed her as a child. Making her father a sandwich and sitting with him on the couch while he watched TV was better than no connection at all. In much the same way, she is preoccupied with setting up the next meeting with her husband or lover, and what she will say or do to keep his interest and approval.

Sharon can also become controlling, eliciting attention with negative behaviors. In this ego state she makes unreasonable demands or throws tantrums if she does not get her way. She may call her husband's other lovers to stir-up trouble. Negative episodes are followed by endless conversations with the various actors, and the high drama maintains a connection to them all, albeit, a painful one. Whether her relationship behavior is fear-based outreach, anxious accommodation, or negative provocation, Sharon's conduct in these regressed states is obviously immature and is viewed by healthier people as irrational and rather ridiculous.

The Feeling that "Something is Missing"

When full awareness of painful feelings was just too much for a child to bear, false selves emerged to help the child survive. The child sent the authentic self into hiding to block true feelings from consciousness. Consequently, as an adult she has a disturbing sense of emptiness and searches externally to soothe the feeling that "something is missing."

An addict longs for a caring relationship, but with any important relationship there are many emotionally loaded interactions that must be managed. Deprived of authentic connection to self, the addict lacks the ability to regulate her own emotions and to navigate relationships successfully. She may make desperate attempts to connect by using old coping behaviors, or may connect with something more predictable than a human being—a mood-altering experience. Addicts end up treating people as objects to be manipulated and controlled sexually to fill their void—a script that healthier people avoid.

The extremes of control—domination and submission—are often incorporated into ritualized fantasy or acting-out scenarios to provide an addict's drug-like high or numbing escape. But controlling or ritualized behaviors do not allow for real intimacy. A fantasy sex partner is merely an object who can readily be replaced by whomever turns up online, at the club, or at the rest stop bathroom. In relationships between addicts and codependents, the need to control each other in an attempt to have one's own needs met may turn into a peculiar game of Dueling Banjos, and efforts to control can escalate precariously.

However, what is "missing" is not the perfect partner or a better sexual buzz. It is the authentic self—the ability to experience a true awareness of self and to connect with one's authentic feelings—the basis from which one can connect well with others. The ability to be accurately aware of one's environment and accept one's genuine feeling-states can guide toward better outcomes.

Help! Get Me Out of Here!—Finding the Authentic Self

Sex addicts generally have no idea that they were wounded by early life experiences, or that what is troubling them most is largely outside of their conscious awareness, or that addiction is really a reenactment of dissociative behavior. They do not know that the "something is missing" feeling is about a lost connection to authentic self, or understand the important role self-awareness plays in relating to others. They do not know that the extreme emotions of shame, terror, and the excruciating pangs of longing to be loved, deeply internalized to survive a painful childhood, are driving their acting-out.

When they begin treatment, addicts are often relieved to learn they have a medical problem that is rooted in trauma. However, mere knowledge of one's trauma does not automatically heal distorted beliefs and feelings embedded at the time of the trauma. The head may learn to say, "It happened a long time ago," but when symptoms are triggered, the body says, "It feels like it's happening right now." Survivors will have to do more than intellectually understand the impact of trauma to overcome their struggle with emotional reactivity, their feelings of shame and fear of abandonment, and their physical, emotional, and visual flashbacks.

Recovery involves learning healthy relationship and attachment skills that addicts did not have the opportunity to learn before. With assistance addicts can excavate the buried authentic self and fill the "something is missing" void. They can learn to distinguish emotions in the present from the over-reactivity of their false selves, and to calm intense emotions rather than act them out self-destructively. By learning to identify their authentic emotions they can gain a greater sense of empathy and self-esteem, and use this internal understanding to guide better decision-making. They can depend on themselves to be more perceptive about others, and to trust them when appropriate to do so. They can develop the ability to maintain a more confident sense of themselves in the presence of others. They can learn to center their lives on more positive beliefs, values, and better thinking, rather than on the feeling-memories and distorted beliefs of sad, scared, lonely children. They can learn to enjoy a variety of healthy relationships with people, rather than cling to those who exploit them or whom they try to control. They will no longer have to substitute addictions for real intimacy in real relationships.

As my client Jerry's treatment progressed, he came to understand the unconscious motivations for his strange behavior. Jerry was repeating the experiences of emotional abandonment he suffered in childhood and the sexual abuse he experienced in adolescence. Tragically, Jerry had been groomed for sex by a former college football coach who ran a day camp for disadvantaged boys. The coach used institutional facilities and a façade of goodwill to cover his serial sodomy of vulnerable children. Powerless and afraid, Jerry had been entangled in a pedophile's web. Now, he was reenacting the painful memories from the past in disguised form. He had lost and was unaware of his authentic self, and was using other people to meet his needs. When he recognized this, Jerry fully committed to his recovery program, and dedicated himself to confronting and resolving the shame he had buried. He wanted to regain a healthy relationship with himself, so that he could have healthy relationships with others.

An integrated treatment program, as described in the previous chapter, which not only helps an addict gain abstinence, but also addresses the dynamics of disrupted development at deeper levels, is usually required to overcome sad life stories that now include addiction. Of all the treatment factors, therapy is the most necessary and important for tackling core identity problems and restoring a proper sense of self. Therapy is needed to adequately resolve the persistent and distressing symptoms of attachment loss and trauma that often lead to relapse.

Excavating the Authentic Self —
Treatment Methods and Tools

Neuroscience and the Biology of Trauma

Theories about the profound impact of loss and trauma based on clinical research and experience are being substantiated by modern neuroscience. The biological consequences of trauma include: 1) having higher levels of certain neurotransmitters created during hyper-arousal (negative neuro-circuits are strengthened); 2) the loss of healthy interaction experiences with caregivers upon which normal neuro-development depends (positive neuro-circuits were not exercised properly and are weakened); and 3) the repression of intense memories that sidetracks energy from the maturation process. Trauma refuses to stay buried because it has a biological impact with enduring effects.

Neuroscience is also validating the efficacy of treatment modalities that address areas in which brain development and functioning were disrupted by trauma. Neuroscience, neuropsychiatry, and psychotherapy are being integrated with implications for treatment of attachment disorders and addictions. Allan Schore, a preeminent expert on the developmental impact of attachment loss, concludes that therapy must be directed toward restoring areas of the brain impacted by trauma. As he highlights, "Because the right hemisphere is dominant for processing social, emotional, and bodily information, the relationally influenced development and organization of this hemisphere has profound effects on a person's capacity for empathy, attention, and coping with stress."[46]

Fortunately, with approaches developed by innovative clinicians and self-help communities, we can address areas of the brain that modern neuroscience confirms are impacted by trauma and loss. Effective methods can help addicts minimize symptoms, reduce their risk of relapse, and gain stability. Some of these methods and the important contributions they make to an addict's recovery will be presented next. This is by no means a comprehensive review, but is intended merely to illustrate the value of a few.

Banished Knowledge

Prior to modern neuroscience, extensive research on attachment loss and the work of many dedicated clinicians revealed that childhood development is profoundly affected by early life experiences, and that early coping mechanisms are carried into adulthood. Alice Miller was one of the first psychotherapists to observe and write about the prolonged physical and emotional effects of childhood trauma. In her book, *The Drama of the Gifted Child: The Search for the True Self,* she explores the phenomena of repressed memories and how they must be treated to diminish persistent symptoms.[47] In order to be in the "present moment," a survivor must confront the truth of what he or she suffered in childhood.

Like Miller, I assist clients in integrating fragmented memories of trauma—images, physical sensations, and distorted emotions and beliefs—and connecting them to the original trauma. This effectively bridges the gap between the feeling-self of the child and the conscious knowing-self of the adult. In this way the trauma survivor can consciously grieve his losses, feel compassion for the innocent and dependent child he was, and finally be free of the debilitating effects of repressed memories. The trauma fades into the background and feels more like a memory should—like something in the past. The adult no longer interprets the present through the warped lenses of an abused child's emotions and distorted core beliefs, or uses the child's coping mechanisms, which have become counterproductive.

As memories are integrated, a survivor's perspective shifts from, "It was my fault because I wasn't good enough," to become, "I was a child dealing with a difficult situation and I did the best I could." In this process the survivor regains self-esteem—the clarity of being in touch with one's own authentic feelings in any given moment and knowing what they are about.

Helping Witness

Miller also recognized that resilient children, those who survived their trauma relatively intact, often had a *helping witness*.[48] This might be a grandmother, teacher, neighbor, or even a pet. The child believed that the helping witness thought well of him and was present to him, even if the matter of the child's harsh circumstances was not mentioned between them. I ask my clients if anyone was "there" for them, because these positive memories, if they exist, are a useful therapeutic resource. When asked to recall such a person, clients will often smile or tears will fall, and they will begin to tell a healing story.

> *In my client Anita's case, "It was my grandfather," she said. "I spent several summers with my grandparents, where I was away from my father's alcoholic rages and sexual abuse. Grandpa just took me with him, whatever he was doing . . . whether it was going fishing, to the grocery store, or working on the car. He seemed to be interested when I talked and he never got mad. He never said anything to me about my Dad abusing me, but I know he didn't like him. He died twenty years ago and I still miss my Grandpa."*

Anita could recall the feeling-experience of someone caring for her as a child, and that connection was an emotional lifeline. Her capacity for empathy and compassion for self, and therefore, the ability to connect in caring relationships, was improved by the memory of her helping witness.

Family Systems and Chronic Anxiety

Murray Bowen, who developed Bowen Family Systems Theory, also contributed to our understanding of the enduring effects of unresolved trauma.[49] He combined his knowledge of biological systems in nature with extensive observation of family interactions. He noted that symptoms of trauma in an adult indicated not only the impact of trauma on that person as a child, but also the impact of trauma on the family system in which that person was reared. He observed that when tragic loss is not adequately grieved, or when addiction or mental illness overwhelms a family, high levels of emotional intensity become chronic. Not only is a child's brain and body chemistry in an ongoing state of hyper-arousal, but also the entire family is hyper-aroused, a condition that Bowen termed *chronic anxiety*.

Bowen also observed that chronically high levels of emotional intensity are cumulative over generations. It manifests in physical, emotional, relational, and behavioral symptoms, including addiction. Symptoms of trauma may be evidenced in later generations even if descendants are unaware there was trauma in their family's past. They will often behave and feel as if they themselves had the traumatic experience. A family system, as well as individual family members, may exhibit symptoms of historical trauma. Unresolved emotional intensity and biologically based coping patterns are transmitted from generation to generation.

Bowen believed that an adult's out-of-proportion emotional intensity in the present, which is often an addict's unconscious reason for escape into his addiction, is usually about childhood and unresolved issues in his family of origin. If a family is already managing chronic anxiety about unresolved issues, emotional intensity can be easily evoked as if an everyday problem is a matter of life and death. Family members are typically dealing with ordinary events of daily life, not crises that warrant a survival response of high anxiety and emotion; normally there is not much reason to "freak out."

The multi-generation family genogram is a standard tool I use at STARPRO to help clients learn important facts about their family history, identify significant unresolved losses and trauma, and understand their addiction in the context of their family system. I encourage careful planning of more thoughtful, adult-like responses, rather than repeatedly getting caught up in the highly intense, emotion-driven patterns that their family had developed to cope in the past. Achieving a differentiated position—emotional functioning that is not dominated by the emotional intensity in one's family of origin—while remaining connected to the family, is key for managing emotions more constructively in relationships beyond the family of origin.

My client, Sarah, was so anxious about the approval of others that she tended to over-accommodate in codependent relationships at her emotional and financial expense. With my guidance, Sarah gathered family history and we constructed a genogram of several generations.

She learned that as a young man, her grandpa lost several small businesses financed by his father. He had numerous brainstorms for making money, but seemed unable to persist with any of his projects. The Great Depression created more challenges for him, but his fighting, gambling, beer, and women also played a role in his lack of success.

Sarah's father, David, became aware at an early age that the family considered his father, Sarah's grandpa, lazy and irresponsible. David felt the shame of his father's failures. He resolved to be more moral and responsible than his father was. David worked long hours, and was eventually very successful in his own business and a pillar of community life. But he always struggled with a feeling that he was never quite good enough, and much like Sarah, over-accommodated others to gain their approval.

During a visit, Sarah's father told a part of Grandpa's story she had not previously heard. Grandpa nearly died in the great flu epidemic of 1918-19. He was eighteen-years-old at the time. He became so ill that his weight dropped dramatically and the family expected his death. They stayed with him around-the-clock. Because of his severe pain, a nurse administered morphine to make him more comfortable.

Grandpa surprised everyone by surviving, but had become addicted to morphine. He battled the disease for quite a while, but after great efforts he overcame it by chain-smoking cigarettes—a habit he never kicked despite two bouts of tuberculosis. Neither he nor his family considered that his ongoing struggles with continual cravings and his unquenchable longing for something to soothe him, were a result of a traumatic life event and the consequences of an unforeseen addiction.

When Sarah learned that Grandpa had struggled with addictive brain chemistry and contemplated the effects that probably had on him, she realized that he might not have been so "lazy." She was proud that Grandpa had made a heroic effort to survive the flu, to get morphine out of his life, and to start some businesses. Sarah also came to understand more about the anxiety of her own father, who had witnessed the fallout of a life of compulsion and financial loss. It must have been an emotional struggle to always try be "good" and to avoid having the same shortcomings as Grandpa.

Sarah discovered that these stories about her family's trauma helped her better understand her own exaggerated anxiety about achieving success and gaining approval, and may have contributed to her own addictive behavior. She understood that some of her intensity may have been acquired by the passing of the family anxiety torch.

Psychotherapy—Healing Through Relationship

Early relationships and the quality of the parent-child attachment have an enduring impact on a child's view of self and others. Children who have a more "secure base"—a sensitively attuned caregiver—fare better as adults in managing difficult emotions and developing relationships than children whose attachment is "insecure"—disrupted by inconsistency, neglect, or abuse. The quality of the attachment they have experienced shapes their subjective interpretation of future experiences, and influences their behavior throughout adulthood.

In relational or inter-subjective psychotherapy a therapist's role, in part, is similar to that of a sensitively attuned parent. Like a good parent, a good therapist pays attention to non-verbal communication to understand emotions and needs. The therapist pays careful attention to a client's posture, facial expression, breathing, and tone of voice. In this non-verbal communication, the client relates traumatic early life experiences that he is unable to put into words because they are, in large part, unconscious.

Just as a parent and child affect one another's emotional and physical states, so do a therapist and client. A therapist incorporating relational techniques is attentive to this reciprocal aspect of the relationship and may share certain relevant thoughts, feelings, or observations generated within the therapy process, while supporting and educating the client in observing, reflecting upon, and sharing his.

As a predicable therapist provides a consistent center of calm, a client develops a more reflective awareness of self and self-in-relationship. He cultivates the ability to think about his feelings and about the possibilities of different perspectives on his experience. Instead of living in the emotionally reactive state of an abandoned or hurt child, he begins to live in the present and can regulate his emotions in a more adaptive way. In this transformative process, the client who did not have a secure base of attachment in childhood, benefits from the experience of healthy attachment and eventually internalizes a secure base within himself. The client is freed from relationship fears and from emotional and sensory memories based in the past. He is free to have a perspective less "embedded" in his early life experience and more congruent with present reality.

Inner Child Work

John Bradshaw and others have developed "inner child work" as a focus for psychotherapy with addictive disorders.[50] I often incorporate the techniques of inner child work into the therapy process to encourage the recalling and grieving of profound losses in infancy, childhood, or adolescence.

Inner child work encompasses many exercises aimed at the right hemisphere of the brain—tasks that foster the creation of the self-acceptance needed to interact with others as a mature adult, rather than as a fearfully guarded, accommodating, or controlling child. These exercises may include guided imagery; the use of childhood photos and toys to connect with a sense of the younger self; and the writing of letters to oneself as a child, offering understanding and reassurance that was not received at the time. The "inner child" may also be invited to write to the adult self about her fears and experiences, which provides the adult an opportunity to actively imagine the child's perspective. A client may be engaged in non-dominant handwriting or drawing, or in the creation of symbolic artwork, to express feelings that are beyond words. When the results of these exercises are shared with compassionate witnesses, a therapist, or other trusted people, the sense of aloneness in suffering can be diminished and the sense of self in the present restored.

These "right brain" exercises also reconnect an adult with the child-self within—her natural creativity, sense of wonder, trust, and playfulness—all of which are traits important to the well-balanced adult personality. The adult can regain her natural self-acceptance and self-worth, and the ability to be open, non-judgmental, loving, and cooperative.

EMDR

Eye Movement Desensitization and Reprocessing (EMDR), developed by Francine Shapiro, is another set of techniques that may be used to address the traumatic split between the wounded child and the self-responsible adult.[51] EMDR is employed in the context of therapy by helping professionals who have specialized training. At each session a specific memory or set of memories is targeted and reprocessed. Using bi-lateral stimulation that may include knee taps, eye movements, or audio signals, memories can often be desensitized. EMDR shortens the time of distressing recall for a client because it requires relatively little discussion of the memories themselves.

This technique appears to stimulate neuropathways that inform the areas of the brain where a child's trauma experience is stored, with the knowledge and perspective of the adult self. The traumatic memory or memory fragments then fade in intensity and no longer disrupt life in the present.

EMDR may also be combined with somatic therapy, which is designed to increase a client's capacity to manage the negative physical sensations that may be evoked by processing traumatic memories. The client develops resources to maintain an optimal state of bodily arousal when encountering frightening early life memories previously buried, or when confronting trauma experienced as an adult.

Cognitive Behavioral Therapy

Cognitive behavioral therapy has also proven effective for reducing relapse in addictions. People who suffer from addiction, depression, and other psychological problems, often have automatic distorted and self-defeating thoughts based on their negative core beliefs. In cognitive therapy, a client and therapist identify the addict's negative thought patterns and the negative consequences to which they lead. The client practices interrupting this habitual thinking and deliberately shifting to more rational thoughts. This leads to healthier responses to emotions and life circumstances.

12-Step Groups

12-Step "work" has much in common with cognitive therapy—a participant is accountable for identifying and shifting self-defeating thoughts and behaviors. For a recovering addict, dedication to a 12-Step or similar group (Sexaholics Anonymous, Sex Addicts Anonymous, Sex and Love Addicts Anonymous, Codependents of Sex Addicts, S-Anon, Codependents Anonymous, and 16 Steps) is an essential component of a viable recovery.

By actively observing and participating in the safe haven and supportive fellowship of group meetings, an addict has the opportunity to practice more mature behaviors—openness, trust, and listening with empathy rather than judgment. Working the steps with a sponsor facilitates an addict's healing process by helping him face past mistakes and take responsibility for current commitments. The addict improves his brain functioning by relating to others who understand the misery of addiction as well as the necessity of personal accountability and empowerment.

Medication

Medication for mood support or anxiety management can often be helpful. Its use may allow an addict to focus more effectively on recovery efforts and have more energy to actively participate in the healing process. The usefulness of medication is evaluated and discussed on a case-by-case basis.

Reclaiming the Authentic Self

In this chapter we have discussed how the authentic self was exiled by trauma and loss in childhood, and how protective ego states did their best to provide shelter, but intrude as maladaptive coping responses in adulthood. Severe life disruption provoked the creation of false selves and led to the "something is missing" feeling, which can result in the intimacy disorder of sex addiction. We have looked at treatment methods and recovery tools that can help an addict excavate authentic self from addiction and trauma.

Unfortunately, trauma does not stay in the past, and symptoms do not give way to time or insight alone. Excavation of the authentic self is an essential part of the journey of recovery. With the help of a strong recovery program, addicts can excavate the authentic self buried by painful experiences and regain a sense of self-worth. They can center their lives on new healthy beliefs, values, and aspirations in the present. They can make more rational decisions. In recovery they reclaim their birthright—the potential for fulfilling relationships with self and others—as well as their own natural creativity, trust, hope, and confidence.

CHAPTER TWELVE

EVACUATE OR RIDE OUT THE STORM?

The Partner's Dilemma

The paradox is that addictive love is an attempt to gain control of our lives, and in so doing, we go out of control by giving personal power to someone or something other than ourselves.[52]

Brenda Schaeffer

A hurricane develops far out in the ocean, moves slowly, and gains intensity over a period of days or weeks. It may be difficult to detect from ashore until it becomes larger and more powerful, but if it makes landfall, it can be devastating and deadly. The storm is an apt metaphor for sex addiction. Not all tropical storms develop into hurricanes or make landfall, nor do all sexual acting-out behaviors become addictions, but both can potentially escalate and create havoc in our lives.

If you suspect your partner is a sex addict, you are in emotional turmoil. You may be wondering, "How do I know if my suspicions are founded?" And if so, "Should I stay or should I go?" In this chapter I present "red flags" and summarize the five categories of increasing severity of sexual behavior problems, from casual use to criminal sex addiction. I explain the betrayal response—the traumatic reaction experienced in the midst of a shocking realization that one's mate is a sex addict and that shared commitment to fidelity and honesty was an illusion. I outline a positive course of action that can help a betrayed partner address her own emotions and needs. I help her answer her difficult question, "Should I stay or go?" by carefully considering several important indicators, including the level of severity of the loved one's problem, and his willingness to seek treatment.

> *In Ellen's case, the hurricane of sex addiction struck with fury. She was shocked into awareness when her husband, Allen, was arrested for soliciting a prostitute and his photo made the front page of the newspaper the following morning. Allen, a prominent businessman and community leader, insisted that this was his first time to hook-up with a prostitute, and that he "just wanted to see what it was like." In fact, he had been frequenting strip clubs and soliciting prostitutes for years, and until now, had successfully concealed his behavior.*

An assessment helped determine that Allen had a severe sex addiction, and treatment was recommended. In retrospect, Ellen realized there were signs of the gathering storm of his addiction. As do many partners, Ellen saw red flags and did not take heed. "I knew, but I didn't want to know," she told me.

> *Annette knew there was a serious problem when she discovered Aaron's trove of romantic emails to other women and his profiles on dating sites. "Is he a sex addict?" she wondered. Aaron admitted that he was feeling lonely and unappreciated, and was amenable to Annette's suggestion of having a professional consultation.*
>
> *Aaron's acting-out was a wake-up call for the couple, but not necessarily indicative of sex addiction. Aaron and Annette were suffering dangerous estrangement because of a "tornado" of marital stress. In the previous four years, they had had three children and Annette's parents had passed away. Allen had also*

accepted a promising new position in a distant city, which meant
a period of separation until Annette and the children could join
him.

After an assessment, which indicated that Aaron did *not* have a sex
addiction, the couple agreed with a recommendation to begin marital
therapy to improve communication and to make caring for each other
and their marriage a higher priority.

Certified Sex Addiction Therapists and other addiction specialists
are trained to evaluate possible sex addictions and other co-existing
disorders, and can provide appropriate guidance. It is wise for a
concerned partner to seek consultation for her own benefit, even if her
significant other is reluctant to participate. Ignoring the warning signs
and waiting to be overtaken by the storm can be catastrophic.

Red Flags of Sex Addiction

In some cases an addict is so skilled at hiding his sexual secrets
that a partner sees little evidence until a crisis hits. More typically, the
partner notices red flags, increasing in number or frequency over time,
or appearing abruptly with the stress of a precipitating event. She may
feel uncomfortable or that something "is just not right," but minimize
her concerns. Some of the red flags a partner may notice in everyday life
include the following:

- An addict may spend considerable time at the computer
  looking at porn or visiting chat rooms, and may be irritable
  when asked to join family activities or when online time is
  interrupted.

- An addict may have unaccounted for absences, or spend
  an inordinate amount of time on extra "work," or assisting
  friends with "projects." This is especially noteworthy if
  these become excuses for missing important family events
  or other commitments.

- An addict may lie about his whereabouts and activities to conceal his secret life with a façade of normalcy.

- An addict may isolate from activities with a spouse or children because they interfere with getting a fix, which has become his overriding need and obsession.

- An addict may have unaccounted for expenditures, ATM withdrawals, credit card charges, secret accounts, excessive phone calls or texts, or receipts for gambling or other entertainment about which his partner was not apprised.

- An addict may be defensive and evasive when asked questions about absences or expenditures. (Covert activities may or may not indicate addiction, but they certainly indicate a relationship problem).

- An addict may make excuses to avoid being sexual with his partner because he is sexually acting-out with others, or using cybersex and masturbation; or, as a result of high-intensity sexual behaviors, he may have developed erectile dysfunction with his partner.

- An addict may pressure his partner to dress or act like a porn star or to engage in other behaviors, regardless of his partner's discomfort or resistance. The addict feels entitled to these preferences and may exhibit anger if not accommodated.

- An addict may break promises to stop or curb sexual behaviors that are offensive to his partner.

- An addict may exhibit "knight in shining armor" syndrome, rescuing other women from "financial" or "relationship" crises.

- An addict may have a history of sexual behavior problems,

such as periods of promiscuity, multiple affairs, arrests for illegal sexual behaviors, or a history of cruising bars and fitness clubs to pick up "dates."

- An addict may make inappropriate sexual comments or tell frequent sexual jokes, and insist on completing them even when others discourage him or show clear disinterest.

- An addict may behave flirtatiously toward inappropriate people such as relatives, children, a friend's spouse, or people over whom he has authority.

- An addict often has a history of other compulsive behaviors such as gambling, substance abuse, and raging.

- STDs that are contracted outside the primary relationship indicate a fidelity problem and possibly an addiction problem, particularly if this occurs numerous times.

Categories of the Storm

Problematic or addictive sexual behaviors can involve many things—fantasy, masturbation, pornography, affairs, the use of escorts and prostitutes, sexual harassment, exhibitionism, power-position relationships, anonymous sex, child molestation, and cybersex. Determining the degree of severity of a sexual problem, based on experiential knowledge or a professional assessment, provides important guidance for a partner in planning her response and in deciding whether to stay or go. The categories of increasing severity of sexual behaviors are:

Category One: Casual Use

The user may occasionally look at porn or go to strip bars with the guys, for example; or in the case of a woman, read romantic novels or visit a chat room out of curiosity. The behaviors are infrequent and the user can easily forego them in favor of other activities. They have little or no negative effect on the quality of work or relationships.

Category Two: Borderline Problem

The user may feel uneasy about his sexual activity, such as flirting online, having sexualized conversations with a co-worker, or watching porn while masturbating. The user is not preoccupied with the behaviors. Periodic use sometimes disrupts work, relationships, or other activities. For example, a couple may argue about a behavior that seems over-the-line to the partner, or the user is occasionally sidetracked from work because of the sexual activity.

Category Three: Problematic Use

Sexual behaviors, which may include engaging physically with other people, have become more frequent and are now a regular part of the user's routine. The user obsesses and fantasizes about acting-out and the anticipated payoff. Normal or planned activities with family or friends may be disrupted. Work productivity may decrease because the user is tardy or inattentive as a result of late night sessions, or because he is using at work. The user is concealing the extent of his sexual activity and minimizing it to himself. His partner may feel hurt or uneasy.

Category Four: Addiction

In this category the addict has the cardinal symptoms of addiction in relation to his preferred sexual behaviors: He is preoccupied with them; he is continuing despite risks of severe consequences; and he is unable to stop. He may be blaming others for his problems. In Category Four, life is lived in the danger zone and is organized around seeking and using. Nothing is allowed to get in the way. Denial about his invincibility may grow more delusional, propelling the addict toward higher-stakes sexual gambles as more intensity is required to get the same effect.

The addiction has become a relationship minefield and is eroding the base of intimacy—honesty, respect, and mutual consideration. The partner may feel degraded or angry about the addict's acting-out, or the time or money drained by the addiction. If the partner does not know about the sexual behaviors, she may feel confused and distanced by the addict's emotional absence or irritability.

Category Five: Sex Addiction with Criminal Behavior

Category Five, the highest degree of sex addiction, includes addicts who engage in criminal sexual behaviors, such as incest, rape, child sex abuse, or using child pornography. Sex addicts in Category Five are severely impaired, and some are violent and dangerous. It should be noted, however, that not all sex offenders are sex addicts; many have other character disorders or impulse control problems that require specialized treatment or incarceration.

Many of us consider child sex abuse the most heinous of crimes. Child molesters may be sex addicts, or just opportunistic molesters who abuse children for a variety of psychological reasons. Some are true pedophiles who have a lifelong sexual preference for children and act this out in the real world. Psychologists or other specialists who are trained in evaluating sex offenders can determine the exact nature of the problem, the risk for re-offending, and the appropriate treatment or other necessary action.

The Betrayal Response—Shock, Denial, and Panic

Just as people in the direct path of a hurricane can sometimes not believe or evaluate the facts and take action, partners experience shock and denial in the face of mounting and incontrovertible evidence of sex addiction. This is a form of traumatic reaction, which I term *the betrayal response*. It involves classic symptoms of trauma—feelings of disbelief, flashbacks to moments of revelation, nightmares, depression, insomnia, anxiety, and self-blame. Whether the realization of betrayal hits all at once or emerges gradually, denial often sets in. Typical denial responses are:

- Feeling the addict's problem is somehow her fault because she is "not pretty enough" or "sexy enough," or some other imagined reason

- Trying to fix the addict's problem by having stern discussions with him, interrogating him, monitoring his smartphone, or being more sexual with him

- Minimizing the acting-out with statements such as, "It only happened once and he was just unlucky enough to get caught," or, "It happened because he was drunk."

- Blaming others such as the affair partner, the female co-worker who filed a complaint, or the buddies who went to the strip club with the addict

A partner's early denial is often followed by panic and anger. Feeling angry as she realizes the extent of the addict's problem is understandable, but some partners escalate into rage and react by confronting and shaming the addict. This is not a good time for the partner to call the addict's parents and friends and tell them about his secrets, or start a revenge affair, or go on a spending spree. It is not the time to hire a private investigator or plan an entrapment, nor is it the time to give in to her sense of victimization and shame.

Because the addict is powerless over his compulsions, berating and condemning him are of no benefit, and may reinforce the addict's sense of shame, igniting the addiction cycle yet again. The betrayed partner's failure to understand the nature of the illness and that she has no control over it, perpetuates her denial and postpones her own healing.

Taking Care of Yourself

If you are the partner who has been betrayed by a sex addict, you may feel that your lifeboat has capsized and you are adrift in the ocean, especially in the first weeks following the realization. It is difficult to think clearly or act wisely when you are in this extremely emotional state of the betrayal response, which may last from a few weeks to several months. It is followed by a stage of grieving, and ultimately, a stage of repair as you focus on your own recovery.

As I cautioned previously, this is not a time to be reactive, but instead, it is a time to find ways to reduce the intensity of your emotions, and to begin to take care of yourself. If you are in a relationship with a violent sex offender, you are in harm's way and self-care begins with removing yourself from the situation. Many communities offer shelter for women and children in abusive relationships, or your pastor, friends, or family members can support you in finding safe haven.

If your partner appears to be in Category Two, Three, or Four, keep your usual routine as much as possible. Routine grounds you in daily realities and reminds you that the whole world has not changed, even though it may feel like it has. Engage in activities that calm you, especially those that you have used previously to de-stress, such as taking a walk, going to a movie, listening to music, reading, or spending time with your children or with a friend.

Avoid dwelling on your fears with everyone who will listen. Instead, find a wise person to talk to who can be objective in light of your distress— someone who will keep your confidences. Helping professionals are often able to do this more effectively than family members or friends who are more emotionally involved. It might be helpful to write down your thoughts, fears, or hopes, and to share them with your friend or therapist. Many communities have S-ANON, COSA, or 16-Step groups for partners of sex addicts, where you can meet others who have been in similar situations and find encouragement.

Educate yourself about the illness of sex addiction by reading a book or talking to a specialist on the subject. This will help you accept the facts that you did not cause the addict's illness and that you can support his recovery but cannot do it for him. Also read about the recovery process for partners like you, the area of your life for which you can take control.

When you have begun to feel calmer and to think more clearly, ask your therapist to assist you in making a response plan. Write your plan down and find an appropriate time to share it with your significant other. When sharing your plan, state your concerns simply. Be direct and specific about your expectations. For example, by stating, "I am concerned that you have a serious problem with sex and expect you to see a therapist." Tell him what action you will be taking on your own behalf in the meantime.

Whether the addict is pursuing recovery immediately or not, you must focus on your own recovery. Ideally, you will seek treatment from a qualified professional and develop a Five Factor Wellness Program for yourself, including the same components as we discussed for the addict in Chapter Ten—Recovery First, Self-Care, Therapy, Support Group, and Meditation.

Why do you need your own recovery? There are many important reasons. It is tempting to stay in denial and organize your life around monitoring or fixing your mate rather than dealing with your own emotional pain. But you need wellness, too. You have slowly adapted to emotional abuse, living with someone who is deceptive and manipulative, who is emotionally unavailable and, quite possibly, blames you for his problems. In addition, you may have come into the relationship with an unhealthy tolerance for emotional imbalance, especially if you grew up in an addictive or abusive family.

It is imperative that you work to heal your own wounds, or, whether you stay or go, you will take your baggage with you and repeat your relationship problem. The self-righteous partner who only wants to blame the addict and sees herself solely as a victim, is doomed to repeat her circumstances.

My Partner is a Sex Addict—Do I Stay or Go?

You may be convinced that your partner is a sex addict and hoping that he will embrace recovery; however, you may also fear another nightmare of betrayal in the future. You may be asking yourself, "Should I stay in this relationship, or should I get the heck outta here?" Careful consideration of several important issues is helpful in making your decision.

First, recognizing the *degree of severity* that I described as Categories One through Five, can assist you in planning your response. If your partner falls in Category Five, sex addiction with offender behavior, you may need to evacuate immediately for the physical and emotional safety of you and your children, just as you would evacuate to avoid a direct hit from a Category Five hurricane.

The addict's *willingness to commit to treatment* and to ongoing recovery is another important consideration. In the case of Category Three or Four, if the addict or problem user is committed to recovery, it is usually recommended that you postpone a decision about leaving the relationship for six months to a year. At that time you can decide whether to remain in the relationship based on your partner's progress in recovery, and your own clearer thinking about your emotional, spiritual, and physical wellbeing.

If your addict partner is in strong recovery, he will have a clear program and keep you informed in an ongoing way. You will not have to speculate about whether your partner is actually recovering, because he will check-in with you about his recovery activities and will demonstrate progress as he develops healthier behaviors and attitudes.

Remember, whatever the level of severity of his addiction, the addict's remorse is not recovery. Do not buy promises that he can quit on his own any more than you would believe that heart disease or alcoholism will resolve on its own. The addict may get angry that you do not trust his promises, but he is in denial about his illness. Treatment and a sustained recovery program are required for the addict's brain chemistry to heal. Pleading and promises have little to do with it.

If you and the addict continue to have a high level of conflict, you may need to live apart for a while—a therapeutic separation—during which you communicate regularly, but less frequently, while each of you is working on your own early recovery. Later, you can begin couples therapy and acquire communication skills to reduce conflict and improve emotional intimacy.

A third important consideration in deciding whether you stay or go is *your own wellbeing*. Implementing a Five Factor Wellness Plan will help you become clearer about whether to remain in the relationship. If the addict gains sobriety, you may choose to stay the course with him and continue to participate in recovery together. If he fails to work a strong program and has relapses, you may decide it is not realistic to expect a stable, faithful relationship with him. Having learned to take better care of yourself, you can make a decision that is based not on fear or anger, but on the reality of what is necessary for your relational health and emotional security. The answer comes from within a calmer sense of self, from your knowledge about addiction and recovery, and from your feelings, observations, and objective conclusions.

It is good news that we can often detect sexual problems by early warning signs—that we can see the storm coming. It is also good news that there are options available if the storm of sex addiction has already landed. With guidance from addiction specialists, partners and addicts can access treatment that is life-giving, rather than wait helplessly for total devastation. Recovery is possible for both the addict and partner. Their relationship may be healed if both are willing to commit to wellness as the necessary foundation for a stable and fulfilling coupleship.

CHAPTER THIRTEEN

CLERGY AND iPORN

Sex Addiction in the Faith Community

I do not understand what I do.
For what I want to do I do not do, but what I hate I do.[53]

The Apostle Paul

D oris, the church secretary, was startled when several porn ads popped up on the screen. Because her computer had crashed, she was using the pastor's to prepare the Sunday bulletin. "Who could have slipped into Pastor's office and used his computer?" she wondered. Doris checked the history and found a long list of porn sites. Some were bookmarked under "Favorites." Her heart pounded as she scanned the history and began to realize the shocking truth. "I can't believe it. Can he really be looking at these?"

Pastor Larry, whom she considered a good friend, had a reputation for his dedication to the congregation. Doris admired him for being available whenever church members called about their troubles. He often stayed late for counseling sessions or to catch up on writing his sermon. Doris felt numb and confused.

"What should I do?" "If I tell the personnel committee, what will happen to Pastor Larry?" "Everyone likes him so much, will they even believe me?"

Faith communities are not exempt from the epidemic of sex addiction. Nearly half of Christians report that "porn is a major problem" in their home.[54] Over a third of women readers of *Today's Christian Women* report they have accessed Internet porn.[55] And perhaps most surprising of all, thirty-seven percent of clergy self-reported having significant problems with pornography, primarily iPorn.[56]

Clergy sexual ethics has been a special area of interest in my practice for many years. I counsel impaired clergy, their staff, and congregations wounded by their pastor's sexual misconduct. I also lead preventive education and training events for clergy and laity about best practices to maintain clergy wellness. What I have observed is that many clergy who act-out sexually genuinely want to serve their congregations, but do not understand the nature of their sexual problems. They feel shameful and make great efforts to conceal their activities. They tend to see addictive sexual misconduct as a personal failing rather than a disorder, and are afraid to ask for help because the response is often punitive to their reputations and careers. Of course, some are simply in deep denial about the fact that they are out of control.

But why do clergy have such significant struggles with sexual behaviors? After all, are they not supposed to be more spiritual and moral than the rest of us? In this chapter I will outline why clergy are susceptible to cybersex and other sexual misconduct, and discuss the profound impact a pastor's misconduct can have on a congregation when it is revealed. I will examine how methods for evaluation and treatment of sex addiction can provide valuable tools for addressing sexual misconduct in the church more effectively and compassionately; and how knowledge about sex addiction and treatment can improve strategies for prevention and early intervention.

Clergy Vulnerability

According to Mark Laaser, founder of Faithful and True Ministries, clergy are more vulnerable to cybersex addiction because "[p]astors typically have unstructured schedules and may spend a lot of time alone."[57] For a lonely, overworked pastor, priest, or rabbi, cybersex is an all too convenient refuge.

For the clergyperson who becomes addicted to cybersex, it is a season in "hell." "Just one more time!" the cyber-demons cry out. The pastor can find himself possessed by sexual images and irresistible urges to return to porn sites and chat rooms, or to engage in even more dangerous activities. With time and escalation the risk of discovery increases, and the pastor's ability to function in his pastoral role and within his own family diminishes. Even if he knows he has a problem, the pastor is usually reluctant to disclose it to anyone or seek treatment. He naturally fears the possible ramifications, especially removal from his ministry.

Clergy are vulnerable to cybersex addiction and other forms of sexual acting-out, not only because their general work life fits the profile, but also for other reasons related to their unique profession and personality type. For starters, men and women who select the ministry are often people who focus on the needs of others to gain acceptance and worth. The ministry provides unrelenting opportunities for this. Clergy teach classes, conduct weddings and funerals, lead worship services, and serve on myriad committees. They inspire fund drives and stewardship campaigns. Members seek their counsel and spiritual support during marital crises and parenting dilemmas, and turn to them in the midst of the illness or death of a loved one. In the event of a disaster, they are looked to for solace and hope. Indeed, many congregations expect their pastor to be "on call" 24/7.

If ministering to the needs of others is a pastor's most important priority, he may neglect personal time for his spouse, family, and himself. When I consult with troubled clergy they often share how powerless they feel over a demanding schedule: "I have to conduct the member's funeral. The family expects me to be there, even if it comes during my vacation." They struggle to set reasonable boundaries at work and allow insufficient time for their own care. They may not set aside time for their own spiritual reflection or prayer, even though they encourage others to do so. The well-meaning pastor can easily become overextended, isolated, and eventually burnt out—conditions that render a pastor more vulnerable to cybersex addiction and other forms of misconduct.

The clergyperson who denies his own need for self-care may eventually grow resentful or lonely, or come to feel undervalued and overwhelmed. His "calling to ministry" feels more like a curse, as emotional and spiritual weariness overtakes him. A brief visit to iPorn may seem like a harmless reprieve from fatigue or loneliness, or a well-deserved "reward" for his efforts, but it can quickly lead to being trapped in an inferno of addiction.

Managing the emotional intensity in the life of the church is another stressful challenge for pastors that may nudge them into sexual misbehavior. As shepherding authority figures, pastors inevitably become lightning rods for the emotional intensity of individuals and groups within a congregation. They may get caught up in counterproductive and exhausting scenarios when factions compete for power and control. Because of their authority and the multiple settings in which pastors interact with members, some congregants may develop very intense positive or negative feelings—as if they are in a singular personal relationship with the pastor. It is difficult for any pastor to navigate hundreds of "relationships." Church members may feel slighted or jealous and become highly critical, or, in the other extreme, may even believe they have "fallen in love" with their pastor. Many lonely clergy have destroyed their careers by entertaining the personal compliments and romantic notions of a parishioner, and becoming intimately involved. While members constantly seek their attention, clergy should not take advantage of the pastoral relationship for their own personal needs, or show favoritism to certain parties. This professional stance, which is important for the health of the congregation, can contribute to a deeper sense of isolation and loneliness.

Clergy are also the only profession specifically "ordained" to do "God's work"—to minister to the spiritual needs of those in their charge. Clergy are presumed to have a special relationship with the Almighty, to act as God's representative, and therefore, are expected to be more invulnerable and infallible. The intensity of his role as pastor and the pressure of lofty expectations may increase a pastor's feelings of inadequacy, and intensify his shame when he harbors sexual secrets.

Lastly, in many religions there is a deep legacy of viewing sexual sin as the ultimate sin, and a tendency to attribute shame to sexuality altogether. For some pastors, this renders forbidden sexual experiences all the more enticing and erotic. When a pastor is entangled in cybersex or other types of sexual misconduct and feels he is failing as a model of morality, religious shame may fuel further motivation to hide the problem—or to cope by escaping "just one more time" to a sexual experience.

The Impact of Disclosure

Over the past two decades we have heard much about clergy sexual misconduct, some of which may be based in sex addiction. Emotional and spiritual shockwaves have been sent through faith communities, and litigation has cost fortunes. Malfeasance among clergy ranges across the continuum of severity, and whether their problems are criminal sex offending, sexual involvement with parishioners, or using pornography, their congregations pay the price.

When a pastor or church leader's sexual misconduct is disclosed, like it was with Pastor Larry's pornography problem, the initial responses of members of the congregation are similar to the betrayal responses of spouses who discover their partner's sex addiction—shock, denial, blame, and shame. "How could our spiritual leader have such a dark secret?" For members who want to believe the pastor is infallible or look to him as a spiritual "parent," and for those who assume he is diligently fulfilling his pastoral duties, it is difficult to believe rumors or allegations.

Racked by denial and disbelief, members may place blame on those who reported the misconduct, disparage victims, and demonstrate anger toward church officials or members suspected of being "out to get" the pastor. Members choose sides, splitting into camps of those who believe allegations and those who do not. Conflicts often emerge between factions, creating hurtful divisions between families. Feuding can even be carried into future generations of congregational life.

I have counseled parishioners who continued to be convinced that their pastor had been maligned and undermined by a staff member or layperson who "blew it all out of proportion," or believed that their pastor was "not allowed to tell his side of the story," years after their pastor was removed for misconduct. Deep denial can persist despite the fact that an official and thorough inquiry was conducted and there is ample evidence of wrongdoing, and sometimes persists even after a pastor admitted what he did. Just as sexual predators may be remembered by their victims as "someone who really cared about me," the pastor who was removed from his ministry may be perceived as having been more "available and caring." A pastor who has poor personal boundaries is often overly solicitous in his need for approval, and excels at being charming. This personality trait aids his efforts to cover-up problems that are already hard to believe.

Unfortunately, much like a spouse or children in an abusive family may take on shame for an abuser's problems, congregations may internalize shame for a pastor's transgressions. They may feel it is somehow their fault. "Maybe we expected too much." "Maybe we should have given the pastor more time off." A pastor who is in denial may also shame the congregation by accusing the victim, or blaming the stress of his job responsibilities. Or, he may create major cognitive dissonance in the church by denying his actions altogether.

For some parishioners, betrayal by a pastor who has been accused of sexual or other misconduct is experienced as a betrayal by God, who "let these bad things happen to us." For others it is a painful reenactment of previous betrayal in a marriage, or of abandonment in childhood. These persons, who were seeking solace and healing trust in the church, may have considerable difficulty reclaiming a spiritual life or confidently returning to a faith community. Usually fallout includes some members leaving the church, disillusioned by what they consider their pastor's moral failings or God's abandonment.

When clergy sexual misbehavior is revealed, all of the parties— the impaired pastor, his family, victims, and the congregation—need support to deal with the trauma. Not unlike a traumatized family, if the congregation buries its pain rather than confronting it, they will continue to carry the symptoms of anger and shame. They may mistrust new leadership and members, experience congregational depression, feel powerlessness and inadequate, or have a damaged identity as a "bad church" that makes its pastors sick or does not protect its members. The congregation is more likely to have difficulty with future transitions. However, if the trauma and loss is concretely identified, grieved and resolved, both individually and also collectively, the church can regain health and resilience and weather the challenges of the future well.

Effective Response

New methods for the assessment and treatment of sex addiction provide valuable tools for dealing with sexual misconduct in the church in more compassionate and effective ways. Trained therapists can assist in determining whether a pastor's sexual acting-out is based in sex or other addiction (such as alcoholism), depression, stress, or other serious psychological problems. An appropriate level of treatment can be recommended, and in some cases—for more "victimless" transgressions—the restoration of the impaired clergyperson to his ministry is feasible. Of course, a small percentage of clergy are sex offenders who are highly recidivistic and require long term intensive treatment. They suffer such serious impairment that is it unsafe and irresponsible to even consider continued ministry. Further, it invites litigation if offenders are appointed to settings in which they may reoffend.

If it is determined that a pastor can safely remain in or return to his position, the personnel committee can establish appropriate expectations for the pastor's accountability as a condition of his continued ministry. The pastor's recovery is supported when he provides the committee with regular updates on his compliance with treatment and progress in recovery. He must be expected to maintain a reasonable work schedule and account for his time. The committee can also require the pastor to schedule vacations and continuing education, and actively encourage family and personal time. It can further support his recovery by assisting him in setting priorities for his ministry, and empowering laity as co-ministers to share responsibilities.

Because a pastor's tasks of ministry are often not visible, church officials can educate the congregation about the many functions of the pastor other than preaching at worship. The congregation can be encouraged to respect the pastor's personal time and call on his designated assistant or lay leader if an emergency arises when the pastor is off. In cases where it is feasible for a pastor to resume his role, the pastor in recovery from sex addiction can provide a powerful and positive model for his congregation, among whom there will be many struggling with similar problems. His own healing may help promote healing in the congregation.

More broadly, a professional consultant can assist in assessing the impact on a congregation and recommend interventions to facilitate their healing as well. Some churches have specialists or "crisis response teams" trained for this purpose. In congregations in which the pastor is removed for sex addiction or sex offending, it is wise to tell the congregation the truth in general terms. A consultant or response team can assist in this process, as well as maintain respect for issues of confidentially, which must be handled delicately. Members need an opportunity to ask questions, vent feelings, and grieve together to prevent conversations and emotions from going underground and sabotaging the future life of the church. When led by trained persons who understand trauma, loss, and grief, these interventions can facilitate congregational recovery.

An excellent resource for further reading on this subject is *Creating a Healthier Church: Family Systems Theory, Leadership and Congregational Life*, which addresses the challenges of dealing with emotional intensity in the life of the church, and provides an invaluable tool for training pastors and lay leadership to respond constructively to crises.[58]

Prevention and Education

Just as a spouse or family may overlook indicators, staff and congregations often overlook or gradually accommodate to signs and symptoms of a pastor's problem. Perhaps there is not sufficient inquiry about rumors of inappropriate or unprofessional behavior, or unaccounted for time. It is difficult for many to believe that the pastor would have a salacious secret life, but sexual problems are rampant in the ministry; and sex addiction among clergy is too consequential to ignore. Fortunately, many denominations and independent churches have already begun to respond proactively to prevent tragedies of clergy misconduct. For churches that have not yet done so, now is the time to begin.

Develop practices that help clergy stay well and avoid isolation and burnout. Invite professionals to conduct special training in clergy boundaries and sexual ethics. Have sexual harassment and sexual misconduct policies, and streamlined procedures for reporting concerns. Carefully screen volunteers and staff, especially those that interact with children. And monitor for the warning signs of sex or other addictions. Use existing channels of communication to educate members about the storm of sex addiction and the threat it poses to individuals and the church.

Implementing preparedness programs can reduce the number and severity of pastoral and congregational problems, and can result in earlier identification of pastors challenged by depression, misconduct, or addictions. Churches should enlist the help of professionals to provide tools for creating a framework of education on clergy sexual ethics, and for proper evaluation, treatment, and crisis management when impaired clergy are identified. Many tragedies can be prevented, and the impact of sexual misconduct better contained.

PART FOUR

FACING THE STORM

CHAPTER FOURTEEN

In the Path of the Storm

Looking Out for Your Family: Part I

Children need time and space, attention, affection, guidance and conversation. They need sheltered places where they can be safe as they learn what they need to know to survive.[59]

Mary Pipher

We can give our children the best preventive medicine against addiction and equip them for healthy lives and relationships. There are Four Principles for building strong family life that will provide shelter from the storm of sex addiction and from social forces that can disrupt our children's development. These principles are Parental Connection, Protection, Respect, and Communication.

Principle One: Connection

Children are remarkably resilient; they sustain trauma well when they have secure bonds with parents, nurturing family, and supportive community. With the assurance that they are loved and cared for by the adults in their lives, they can heal from the searing wounds of tragic loss. They can direct their energy to age-appropriate activities, academic progress, and the social experiences needed for maturation. When vital resources are available, they are likely not only to survive, but also to thrive.

But when the guiding light of parental empathy is extinguished and the nurturing connection to family and community is broken, children are at risk. When they are stranded in the strike zone of parental addiction or other trauma, they are forced to bury their feelings and redirect their energy to survival. They are more vulnerable to negative external influences and to attachment to something other than relationships for comfort.

Stranded in the Strike Zone—Jerry's Story

When Jerry was eight-years-old his father was permanently disabled by a back injury and had to give up the job he loved. Confined to the house, what had previously been problems with alcohol and pornography, soon became addictions. As his parents' marriage collapsed, Jerry's mother turned to him for emotional support. Jerry lost his birthright to be nurtured and protected as a child, and instead became his parents' caregiver.

Jerry felt sorry for his father who spent most of his day drinking on the living room couch. He missed the days before his dad's accident when they played catch or wrestled. He dreaded going home after school to help out, which, before his parents' divorce, included stashing Dad's porn videos out of his mother's sight. "Your mom doesn't like this stuff around," his dad would say. Often, Jerry could hear his parents arguing about his dad staying up to watch sex videos late at night.

Jerry felt sorry for his mother, too. She talked to him about financial worries and complained bitterly that she "didn't have fun anymore" because his dad could no longer play golf or socialize. As a teenager Jerry agreed to take dance lessons and be his mother's partner on Friday nights at the dance club where she and his father used to go. This meant giving up Friday night activities with friends of his own.

Jerry felt trapped and inadequate. His dad needed physical assistance, and his mother was relying on him for adult emotional support. Jerry felt guilty for secretly resenting his sacrifices. He felt shame about his own need to be loved. His longing for attention and caring was exploited when Jerry was groomed by a skilled sexual predator.

As an adult, Jerry sought therapy for his own sex addiction. In treatment he began to understand that he consciously longed for love, but unconsciously was reenacting his trauma. He was seeking the lost empathetic connection with his parents. He unknowingly set up sexual scenarios that replayed his anxious longing to be noticed, and which provided sporadic gratification when he offered himself to satisfy someone else's needs. His encounters were always followed by a familiar loneliness and shame.

Jerry became aware that while he could be physically intimate, he avoided being emotionally intimate, fearing that others would expect too much from him. His acting-out with sex prevented him from risking real vulnerability. He had developed an intimacy disorder. He did not know how to connect.

Stranded in the Strike Zone—Jennifer's Story

Jennifer was alone and adrift on an emotional island created by forces beyond her control. She was abandoned by her father at age three and left in the custody of her mother, a sex addict and alcoholic who was immersed in the preoccupation and rituals of her addictions. At six-years-old Jennifer was getting herself up in the morning, dressing, and going to school while her mother slept in with her latest lover. The lovers changed so frequently that Jennifer could not remember most of their names.

Her mother often went out for the night, leaving Jennifer to warm a can of soup for her supper and to put herself to bed alone. Jennifer learned to clean house, do laundry, and buy groceries at the corner store. She also learned to expect scant attention to her needs and to block out feelings of loneliness and fear.

Jennifer saw extended family once or twice a year at holidays. She was painfully aware that she and her mother were treated as outsiders. The little cousins stared and went off to play without her, while the adults made condescending remarks about her mother's lifestyle. Because of her mother's frequent job changes they relocated often, so Jennifer's connections to friends were also tenuous until she was fourteen, when her mother got a steady job with a new boyfriend's company.

Jennifer found a substitute family in high school—a group of lonely children who looked out for each other and experimented with alcohol and sex. Jennifer discovered sex and alcohol helped her feel "happier," at least temporarily. She became increasingly self-conscious and was embarrassed how shabby her clothes and home appeared, relative to those of her more affluent friends. Jennifer vowed to get a good job someday and have nice things of her own. She poured herself into studying and enjoyed the recognition of being a "straight-A" student. She developed a work compulsivity that allowed for some success. Whereas many would have devolved into an under-functioning state, she managed her feelings by over-functioning. She was able to support herself through college with academic scholarships, a part-time job, and student loans. But she still found time to party, escalating into heavy binge cycles and extreme sexual promiscuity.

Jennifer completed her degree and shortly thereafter married Dave, a handsome young man with a strong career. It seemed he had a stable, intact family—at least compared to hers. Unfortunately, Dave was controlling and had a violent temper. Jennifer overlooked these red flags; she had learned long ago to be pleasing and to ignore her own feelings. She failed to heed her personal experience and others' warnings about Dave's potential for aggressive drama.

Because she expected so little for herself, Jennifer was the ideal choice for the type of marriage that was familiar to Dave—one like his parents'—in which the children did as Father commanded, and Mother did not express her thoughts or feelings. For years Jennifer endured her husband's neglect of her needs, and his physical abuse of her and their children. She often felt shame, as if she had done something wrong to cause his outbursts.

I first met Jennifer when her oldest child showed signs of depression. Jennifer, motivated by her desire to be a good parent, brought her daughter to see me. She suspected her husband's domineering behaviors were taking a serious toll on the children. Jennifer listened intently as her daughter poured-out her pent-up anger about "Dad constantly yelling and hitting us," and about her mother "just letting him."

Jennifer scheduled sessions for herself, at first to talk about her children, but gradually she revealed her own feelings. Jennifer had navigated the shoals of her parentally disconnected childhood, but she was deeply wounded. She realized she was allowing herself and the children to be abused, but she felt helpless to do anything about it. She wanted help providing safety and a loving environment for her children. She did not want them to live with the same emotional pain that she had experienced. But at the mere thought of confronting Dave, she felt flooded with fear that he would abandon her.

In the course of her therapy Jennifer began to see that she was essentially re-enacting her childhood, including the misperception that the situation is her fault, and the feeling that she is helpless and should just trod along. She began connecting her emotions to the past trauma where they originated, and grieving the losses of her childhood. She found many inner resources, including memories of a neighbor with whom she had been allowed to spend a little time—someone she recalled as having been very positive and kind to her. Memories of her neighbor's empathy and caring became a healing reminder that she needed kindness and respect as a child and, likewise, as an adult—and that her children needed those things, too.

When Jennifer felt safer within herself, she was able to proactively address her marital problems and to be more intuitive about the needs of her children. She learned to live a life more consistent with her best thinking and values, and to model and provide a healthy home. Though she had endured attachment loss and hardship, creating and maintaining a strong parental connection with her own children—to give them what she never had—became a paramount objective, and she was successful.

Clean Up Your Own Mess First

Any childhood trauma can have a detrimental effect on a child's sense of loving connectedness. When a parent suffers from an addiction, including sex addiction, the children will suffer too. Having an addicted parent will blow holes in a child's life raft of family stability and parental connection. For children whose parents are addicts, it feels like a dark night in a never-ending storm. The damage inflicted is devastating. As their parent's addiction progresses, their world collapses around them and they are robbed of vital resources for healthy development. When parents are addicts there is no place to hide, because addicts are emotionally dysfunctional and their addiction pervades their relationships. The situation grows direr for a child when an addiction and its fallout sever connections with extended family, friends, neighbors, and a broader community.

Many resilient children who experience neglect and trauma can survive and function remarkably well in adult life, yet many sustain wounds that derail their emotional and relational lives. Among other things they struggle with self-esteem, and with mood disorders such as anxiety and depression. They find it difficult to trust others or to feel their needs and wants are valid. These symptoms impair their ability to have rewarding intimate relationships and make them vulnerable to bad relationships or addictions as substitutes.

Therefore, the first order of parental connectedness is to clean up your own mess, first. Get help with any addictions you have; seek help to deal with your past trauma; learn to be kindly conscious of your children; interact with them in a way that ensures they do not sustain trauma; and love them and protect them from negative influence.

Sheltered from the Storm—Janie's and Michael's Story

In contrast to the stories above, Janie and Michael have the parental connection and community support they need at a time of tragic loss.

Janie, age eight, and Michael, age ten, had a terrible summer. Their father, Ed, died at age forty-two, one year after he was diagnosed with lung cancer. Janie and Michael watched as their strong, handsome father dropped fifty pounds, became so weak he had to quit his job, and finally was unable to walk without assistance, or feed and bathe himself.

The untimely death of a parent is one of the most traumatic losses a child can sustain. Janie's and Michael's hearts are broken, and they are grieving deeply. They have difficulty sleeping and want to stay close to Mom. They are sad, and at times angry, but more often in a fog of disbelief. However, we can predict that Janie and Michael will begin to heal because they have invaluable resources—strong bonds with their parents, a supportive family, and a nurturing community of friends, neighbors, and teachers. These resources will sustain them through their trauma and grief. In time, they will resume their activities with their former enthusiasm. In fact, we can predict that Janie and Michael are likely to fulfill their potential to become emotionally healthy, successful, and loving adults.

Janie's and Michael's most vital assets are the nurturing connections they have with both parents. Although their father is no longer alive, his emotional bond with them continues through the countless experiences they shared and in the values they learned from him. Ed was very involved in his children's daily lives. He played and worked with them, loved and encouraged them, and provided consistent parental guidance. He taught them that you do not get paid for every favor done for a neighbor—sometimes you just mow their lawn for the satisfaction of helping others. Because he was a loving father, they will always have had a loving father, and this will be a guiding light in their lives. They will see themselves as they were reflected in his eyes—smart, capable, and loveable.

Laurie, their mother, is also a priceless asset. She encourages the children to express their emotions and responds with acceptance and reassurance. Of course, Laurie is also grieving, and she has turned to supportive friends and family in the difficult transition to life without

Ed. They help her by doing practical tasks such as home repairs or errands, having the children over so she can rest, and listening when she needs to talk.

I asked Laurie how she and the children are doing. "It's hard for all of us," she said. "Michael wants to act like everything is the same, but he has cried a few times and said, 'I wish Dad was here.' And Janie is having tantrums over little things almost every day." Laurie knows that children should not be expected to "hold it together" in the midst of deep loss, that in fact they need to "fall apart" at times, and be comforted by adults.

Tears came to her eyes as she continued sharing, "They don't want to talk too much about their dad, so I bring up things he used to say or I ask how they are doing with missing Dad." Laurie continued, "In a couple of weeks I want to make a memory book with the kids. We'll put in family pictures and stories about favorite times with Dad, that kind of thing." Laurie understands that repressed grief can lead to depression or behavior problems later, so she is letting them know that talking about Dad and being sad is okay. Laurie and I have discussed how children often blame themselves when a parent dies and sometimes feel that they were abandoned. She reassures her children that Ed's illness was not their fault, and tells them how much he loved them—and how much she loves them, too.

Fortunately, several members of the extended family live nearby and Janie and Michael often spend time with them. Michael's uncle takes him golfing and they do yard work together, like Michael and his father did. And Janie was excited to tell me recently, "We're going on a family trip to Colorado with my aunt and uncle, and cousin," and that she had earned extra money for souvenirs by doing chores for her aunt.

Bea and Harlan, their neighbors next door, have become like grandparents to Janie and Michael. Harlan shared afternoons on the patio with Ed in his final months. Bea and Harlan invite Laurie and the children to join them for meals, and the children are welcome to drop by after school to play pool or just hang out. The security and love of their mother and extended family, and friends like Bea and Harlan, are helping Janie and Michael heal. They are ensuring connectedness.

Although they are experiencing trauma, within this healthy support system Janie and Michael will continue to develop a sense of self-worth and to believe that others will be there for them. Janie and Michael are learning they do not have to "go it alone," and that with the help of others they can make it through the most difficult of times. They have vital resources including encouragement to express their emotions, the involvement and support of extended family, professional counseling, healthy connections to friends, neighbors, and community, and most importantly, a nurturing connection to their parents.

Family and Community

In this day and age, family life is shaky or non-existent as parents struggle with chaotic schedules and the pressure to make enough money to provide material things. Cyberspace, consumerism, and excitement often become substitutes for family, neighborhood, and nature. Parenting is piled on the strained nuclear family, or on the single parent often living at a distance from extended family. It is all the more difficult to remain committed and connected, but all the more important to try.

> *"Ryan is really a good kid, but lately, he doesn't want to do anything except watch TV. I think he's depressed," reported Sonya. She and her fourteen-year-old son were seated on the couch in my office for their first appointment. As I talked to Ryan and his mother, I discovered that Mom, Dad, and Ryan were living separate lives in the same house. They ate meals alone, and spent evenings and weekends largely in solitary activities in separate rooms.*
>
> *"I wonder if Ryan's depression might have something to do with feeling lonely and disconnected," I said. Ryan looked up at me. With sadness in his eyes, he nodded his head in agreement.*

Unfortunately, this is a common scenario in American family life. Family time is trumped by outside activities or tech devices in the home. Sadly, in cases like that of Ryan's family, being disconnected feels "normal" to parents who grew up in emotionally disconnected families themselves. Even fairly well-adjusted families spend less time together, have less eye contact, and have less frequent "welcome home" greetings than previous generations. When shared family activities are crowded out, what is most essential to a child's wellbeing and self-esteem—a sense of connection—is sacrificed.

Activities and rituals such as a family meal, a family night, holiday traditions, doing chores or projects together, are essential for a child's emotional security and social development. Activities that provide interaction are especially important—taking walks, cooking a meal together, or playing a game. A child's relationships within the family become his operating manual for future relationships. All of the outside activities—sports, music lessons, and spending time with friends playing video games—may be enjoyable and worthwhile, but are not wholly essential, like a connection to caregivers is.

Extended family time is important, too. Parents should stay in touch with as many of their extended family and close friends as possible. After all, we are mammals designed to thrive in groups. Knowing relatives adds depth to a child's sense of security and, thus, makes him less vulnerable to addiction and social pressure. A relative's annoying personality, occasional disappointments, or grudges over the past should not become more important than "sticking together" as a family.

In former times, the responsibilities of raising children were shared by a village of relatives, friends, and neighbors who interacted with each other in the community. In her book, *The Shelter of Each Other: Rebuilding Our Families*, Mary Pipher describes growing up in a small Nebraska town in which everyone knew her name, and looking out for children was a shared effort.[60] She recalls the day she stole lilacs from a neighbor's yard without permission, and how news of it reached her parents before she arrived home. She learned that her actions were known to others and that she could expect to be held accountable. As the story exemplifies, such experiences instill positive values and contribute to children's development of conscience. Knowing they will be seen and recognized by others, the "fishbowl effect," helps guide their social behavior.

On the other hand, when children grow up feeling anonymous or invisible, they are more likely to believe that, "Nobody knows, so it doesn't really matter what I do." Being lovingly connected to family and community, and having a life with consistency and a predictable sense of security, will help insulate our children from negative emotions and detrimental choices. They will have a shelter from the storm.

CHAPTER FIFTEEN

IN THE PATH OF THE STORM

Looking Out for Your Family: Part II

The child wants simple things. It wants to be listened to. It wants to be loved.... It may not even know the words, but it wants its rights protected and its self-respect unviolated. It needs you to be there.[61]

Ron Kurtz

Building on the critically important foundation of Parental Connection, additional Principles for strong family life are Parental Protection, Respect, and Communication. These too will provide shelter from the storm of sex addiction and from confusing and disruptive cultural messages.

Principle Two: Protection

To become healthy adults, children, first of all, need to be children. Protecting children from experiences for which they are not emotionally or socially ready, and from products that will rob them of an innocent childhood, is our responsibility as parents and caregivers. It is vital that we set protective boundaries and provide direction. This includes setting limits by establishing clear expectations, rules, and consequences—including in cyberspace; and by practicing moderation and restraint in materialism.

Setting Limits with Expectations, Rules, and Consequences

Protecting our children's development involves appropriate expectations, rules, and consequences. These provide a sense of security that is fundamental to a child's emotional wellbeing. They also teach important life lessons—that there are consequences for poor behavior, and that respect for authority and consideration for others is generally helpful. When expectations, rules, and consequences are clarified and regularly enforced by parents without much fanfare or debate, theatrics calm down and cooperation increases. Expectations may include household chores, regular bedtime, attitudes of respect and cooperation, or time limits on tech devices.

It is important that parents decide together what the expectations, rules, and consequences will be, so they can genuinely support one another's authority in these areas. Mom and Dad can listen respectfully to a child's suggestions, but parents have the final say. When expectations are clear, the child can choose to cooperate or not, and experience the consequences—much like adult life. If parents are separated or divorced, each needs to support the parental authority in the other's household. One parent undermining another sabotages parenting effectiveness. Nuances of parenting style are less important than providing parental predictability and instilling a healthy respect for boundaries.

It is by experiencing rules and consequences in the family that a child will develop his own internal rules for conducting his life. This is a gradual maturation process that requires patience and consistency on the part of parents and caregivers, as well as encouragement for a child to make the right choices at each stage of his development.

Setting Limits in Cyberspace

Children and adolescents are more tech savvy then their parents;

however, they do not have the life experience and judgment to make wise and safe choices online. Their innate curiosity and naiveté put them at risk. We can allow children and adolescents to enjoy the advantages of the Internet Age, but also protect them from the inherent dangers. The following guidelines protect children and also protect family life from the over-intrusion of tech devices:

1. **Tech "Time Outs."** I encourage parents to call regular tech "time outs," which means tech devices of all types are turned off for a specified period of time to allow family interactions to take priority. When parents implement tech time outs regularly (like during the dinner hour), they protect their child's need for emotional connection to the family. I also recommend that all tech devices be parked outside a child's bedroom, which should remain a quiet place to read, expand a hobby or creative interest, or sleep.

2. **Permission and Time Limits.** Problems can be avoided if parents establish a "permission required" rule and time limits related to tech activity. Children will over-indulge in television, the Internet, texting, or gaming when there are no constraints. Designating a half-hour for social networking, or an hour for TV or gaming, for example, creates mindfulness of use and prevents other healthy activities from getting crowded out.

3. **Who, What, Where and When.** Before giving children permission for activities outside the home, good parents expect to know where they are going, who they are going to be with, what the activity is, and when they will return. The "Who, What, Where and When" rule is equally important for safety in cyberspace. What is the purpose of the online session? Where is the child going online—homework, games, or social media? Who will they be interacting with, and when are they expected to be offline or "back home"? Facebook and Twitter accounts should be set up as private, not public. And yes, you should be a

"friend" of your child on Facebook and a "follower" on Twitter. Make sure you know who your kid's social media "friends" are; it is the quality, not the quantity that matters.

4. **Monitoring Tech Activity.** Computer and tablet screens should be visible in the household trafficways at all times, rather than parked in a child's room or an isolated area. Parents can more readily monitor time limits and make random checks to curb the child's normal, but potentially dangerous online curiosity and impulsivity. Most porn viewing and romance chatting by children occurs while they are doing "homework" online. Routine checks of computer history, flash drives, smartphones, and other communication and media devices are in order, as are consequences for infractions. Do not allow secret passwords for anything.

5. **Personal Information Prohibited.** Personal information can be accessed and exploited if provided online. Unfortunately, once given, this information remains in cyberspace forever. We must teach our children that it is not safe to provide personal information under any circumstances, and to report to us if it is requested.

6. **No Blame Reporting.** Encourage children to report any experiences that make them feel suspicious or uncomfortable, and assure them that you will remain calm even if they made an unwise choice of some kind. Sexting, bullying, the solicitation of a minor, or the transfer of explicit images of an underage child, are actionable items. Crimes should be reported to law enforcement.

7. **Protective Software.** Software programs designed to filter or monitor material that is inappropriate for children are available, such as the Mobicip Safe Browser. These must be installed and updated regularly and cannot be relied upon as a sole firewall,

but they are helpful. Screening services are also available from your Internet Service Provider, and screening apps can be obtained for most tech devices.

8. **Discuss Internet Pros and Cons.** Because the Internet and tech devices are ubiquitous in daily life, we frequently have opportunities for conversations about safe practices. An excellent way to start a discussion with a young person is to ask him or her to be the "expert" and to help us assemble a Facebook page, download music, or assist with another project. When we approach tech opportunities with interest, we open the door to further conversations about tech safety issues or other life problems that may arise. Many websites feature engaging videos, music, and games, which are designed for young children and parents to learn together about safe Internet use.

9. **No "Dates" Without Parental Approval.** Children use the term "friend" for any person with whom they are associated online. Children are generally trusting and do not consider that their "friend" may not be who he says he is, or that he could be a stranger who may put them at risk. Therefore, we must inquire whether a friend they are getting together with in the real world is a "real" friend, or a virtual "friend" they met online. Actual meetings or dates in the real world with online "friends" must be approved and supervised by parents. Secret meetings are high risk behavior that merit closer monitoring or limiting of tech devices.

10. **Encourage Face-to-Face Relationships.** When too many of a child's friendships are conducted primarily online or through tech devices, he or she will miss out on opportunities to develop important social skills. The spectrum of communication is narrowed because it lacks non-verbal aspects, such as facial expression, body language, tone, and cadence. These non-verbals carry more information than words alone, and learning

this "language" is necessary for healthy relationships. These skills are acquired by relating to family members, peers, and adults in a variety of face-to-face interactions, not by engaging through technology. Real relationships are far more challenging and intricate than online relationships but, ultimately, more rewarding.

Setting Limits by Practicing Moderation in Materialism

In our materialistic culture, parents often feel compelled to provide their child with the latest tech gadgets, toys, and entertainment—especially the ones his peers have (at least according to him). Parents may experience guilt if they cannot afford popular items, and under pressure, they may spend more than they reasonably should.

It is normal for children to want things and want them "now," whether it is good for them or not. As parents, we must exercise good judgment and set limits. Saying "no" despite a child's complaints demonstrates that we are more interested in the child's wellbeing than in pacifying her for our convenience. Children sense this caring, even when they protest. Moderation, delayed gratification, earning something by effort, and unselfishness are valuable life skills missed if there is overemphasis on material things or instant pleasure. In his bestseller, *Emotional Intelligence: Why It Can Matter More Than IQ,* Daniel Goleman suggests that having the coping skills of frustration tolerance, delayed gratification, and consideration for others may be more important in life success than high IQ.[62]

Responding to a child's emotional needs and giving her time, attention, and love has much more enduring benefits. Who was a person who had a positive impact on your life as you were growing up? Was it someone who was interested, listened, and connected with you and made you feel affirmed and soothed, or someone who merely gave you things? When a child experiences the nurturance of an adult's sincere interest and comforting presence, she is less likely to look for superficial substitutes outside the family.

Principle Three: Respect

I often hear complaints that young people are disrespectful toward parents or other authority figures. We tend to view this as the child's or teenager's problem, but we overlook how we as parents and adult role models contribute. Dismissive language ("whatever") and cruel humor are prevalent these days. Adults spew intolerance and celebrities glamorize disdain and ridicule. It is not surprising that these same elements are displayed in children's bullying. But respect for self (self-esteem) and respect for others are important components of an internal guidance system for making healthy choices and for connecting to healthy people. Parents can model respect by practicing it towards self, the child, and others.

Respect for Self

Parents can most effectively teach children respect for self by modeling it in their own lives. Children learn lifelong lessons, not only from how they are treated, but also from observing how parents treat themselves. They generally follow in our footsteps. Simply put, "If my parents believe they are worthy of self-respect and self-care, then I must be, too."

Most of us can improve our role-modeling in the area of self-respect by examining our lifestyles and priorities and getting them in line with our true physical, emotional, and spiritual needs. We can ask ourselves, "Am I modeling self-respect by caring for my own basic needs, getting enough sleep, eating healthfully, and having some fun?" "Am I modeling self-neglect by neglecting my health, over-working, over-spending, by spending too much time on the Internet, or by indulging an addiction?"

Sex addiction is an extreme form of modeling self-neglect and self-deprivation because it ultimately steals everything of value from an addict, including healthy relationships with his children. If a parent suspects he has an addiction, sexual or otherwise, seeking help is an act of self-respect and an act of love and respect for his children.

Respect for the Child

The principal of respect is reinforced by consistent respect toward a child from his parents. Positive tone of voice, body language, eye contact, and interest in the child's activities and feelings are messages to the child that he is worthy, safe and secure, and that his needs deserve consideration.

Showing appropriate disappointment for a specific misbehavior is a normal reaction from a parent and part of a child's learning about limits. It should be directed toward the behavior ("I'm angry because you did not come home on time."), rather than toward the child's character ("You are a bad boy."). All parents have lost patience on occasion, but if this becomes a pattern, it is not only disrespectful, but abusive. Chronic degrading sarcasm, explosive anger, contempt, and blaming are emotional child abuse.

Because of the high divorce rate, many children experience this unfortunate trauma, which strikes at the core of their security system. Other children have never had an intact family. Regardless of their circumstances, children need both parents to remain positively and actively involved in their lives. It is vital to a child that his parents demonstrate respect for this need and make good on the promise. Putting aside former relationship issues or hostilities and co-parenting respectfully is possible, and is invaluable in protecting a child's self-esteem.

Respect for Others

A human tendency is to divide ourselves into "us" and "them." It is easy to polarize around differences. "We are good; they are bad." "We are right; they are wrong." This kind of thinking leads to objectifying others and to detrimental conflict in the family, in the community, and beyond. Parents can temper this tendency by the attitudes they model. Children learn how to manage differences respectfully (or not), primarily by watching their parents and other adults. If we insist that our way is the one and only way, and vilify those who disagree, this is what our children learn. If we disagree respectfully and are willing to seek mutual solutions, our children can learn the important life skill of respect for others, even though people may see things differently—a circumstance they will frequently encounter in life. Respect for others provides the basis for cooperation and mutuality—tools needed for successful relationships. It also provides the basis for respecting the sexuality of others.

Principle Four: Communication

Communication is the fourth important principle of strong family life. Affirming communication is more effective than negating or controlling communication, and translates directly into self-esteem for our children. An affirming communication style is based on listening, positive responses, and low emotional intensity. Conversely, a controlling communication style is based on talking more than listening, discounting responses, and high intensity interactions such as lecturing and arguing. When parents practice an affirming style their relationships with their children can improve quickly.

Listen and Affirm

Listening is the ultimate communication because it demonstrates interest and regard, and it calms and connects. Unfortunately, most of us are poor listeners. We lecture, interrupt, and push advice, rather than listen. The most frequent complaint of children and adolescents I work with is, "My parents don't listen."

Interestingly, parents tell me they do listen, because they believe they do. However, when I ask a parent to relate a recent example of a conversation with their child, it often becomes clear that the parent delivered a lengthy exhortation, or a "you should," or "you shouldn't," monologue. The parent means well and believes he or she is providing guidance, but is often parenting with a style learned from their own parents—lecturing, rather than listening and conversing.

I frequently coach families on a communication model that emphasizes the skill of listening, and deemphasizes the need for absolute agreement. The "magic" of this model is in the listening, which is demonstrated by letting the speaker know that he or she was heard and understood. This is accomplished by repeating what was said and noting the emotions that were conveyed. After taking turns listening, each person has an opportunity to say what would be helpful to him or her, and mutual solutions can be found more easily. As I coach parents and children through this model, there are often smiles and tears of relief as they connect by listening, and realize that they care about each other, even if they disagree on certain things.

Parents will undoubtedly disagree with their children on many subjects, but listening calmly, even when they disagree, is constructive and healing. When this happens, children feel they were heard and their emotions were respected, even if a parent has to say "no" sometimes.

Reduce Intensity

Yelling, lecturing, nagging, threatening, and arguing are intense communications that are negating and critical and are, frankly, ineffective. High-intensity communication may be effective in the military, but in the family it evokes resistance and resentment rather than cooperation. It can set off a cascade of brain chemistry that causes listening and thinking to diminish.

Children will understand more easily and be more cooperative when parents lower verbal and emotional intensity. When parents can both listen respectfully and also de-intensify communication, relationships with their children will improve. When we, as parents, refrain from "going ballistic" over little things, children will trust us with the big things. If we are too angry or intense, they will confide in and seek comfort from somebody else, somebody who may not have their best interests at heart.

Initiate Conversation

Conversation, the casual exchange of ideas, feelings, or everyday experiences, is the most natural way to affirm a child and teach basic relationship skills. It allows parents to tune in to the child's world. Conversations may be initiated by simply asking what the child thinks or feels about something encountered in the course of everyday life. "What did you think about ___?" "How did you feel about___?"

If an unusual event occurs in a child's day, it is an opportunity to ask questions that invite sharing. Even very young children can converse about their observations, experiences, and feelings. For example, a parent might ask, "What do you think about what James did at school this afternoon?" or, "How did you feel when he shouted at the teacher?" Listening to a child's perspective, rather than critiquing it, will promote more conversation. As the child matures the topics will mature also. But if the habit of conversation is established, "talking things over" will already be in the child's repertoire of skills as his world expands and he encounters new and more complex situations.

Discuss Sexuality

Protection from cybersex, sex addiction, or sexual exploitation is enhanced by having conversations with our children about sexuality. I encourage parents to dialogue openly with their children about sex and relationships from an early age, in ways and about matters appropriate to the child's stage of development. *Talking to Your Kids About Sex*, by Mark Laaser, is an excellent resource.[63]

Tweens and teens are very curious about sexuality, but they are reluctant to talk about it, especially if they sense a parent is uncomfortable with the topic. If a parent ventures to bring up the subject, children will often reassure the parent that they "already know about it" or "learned all about that in school." They may have learned about STDs or reproduction, but little about courtship, romance, and healthy sexuality. Meanwhile, they are bombarded by the media with a "pornified" style of relating to the opposite sex—a poor model for successful intimate relationships. They long for helpful information and direction from adults they can trust. When working with adolescents in therapy, I give them permission to ask questions about sexuality and to talk about their relationship experiences, good or bad. When they trust that the conversation is confidential and the adult is not embarrassed by the topic, they are often eager to do so.

It may be difficult to subdue our own emotions and be present for our children when scary issues come up, especially issues about intimacy and sexuality. However, if we practice listening, keep our intensity down, and respect our child's opinions and emotions, we can become our child's most reliable resource. With a good relationship and open communication, your child will come to you when things are going well, and also when he senses that something is wrong. Listen and be perceptive. If he says, "If you are wondering why my hair is wet, it's because Coach and I took a shower," he is trying to tell you that something does not feel right.

Practicing a respectful exchange of thoughts and feelings with a child creates a template for his future relationships. Using a style of affirming communication, we can give our child a lifelong relational security system—the ability to have caring relationships in which difficult issues can be discussed openly and respectfully.

Four Principles—Preventive Medicine

In these last two chapters we have discussed the Four Principles of strong family life—Parental Connection, Protection, Respect, and Communication—by which we can shelter our children from the storm of sex addiction and invest in their future wellness. Positively connecting with our children can insulate them from trauma. Sharing family activities and being involved in community life can provide for a child's deepest need—a sense of belonging. Establishing clear expectations, rules, and consequences for a child's behavior, setting guidelines for the safe use of technology, and practicing moderation in consumption, can provide protection and security and teach important life skills. Modeling respect for self, the child, and others, strengthens a child's self-esteem and teaches tolerance for diversity of opinion and respect for all persons, including respect for others' sexuality. Practicing an affirming style of communication and listening to understand opens a lifeline, and helps a child develop a solid sense of self and learn important relationship skills. The child does not have to search for information or comfort elsewhere.

Building strong family life based on the Four Principles—Connection, Protection, Respect, and Communication—requires regular investment of parental time and energy, but it pays high dividends. Not only do we immunize our children against sex addiction and negative sex messages, but we also equip them with the life skills necessary for their future relationships and personal wellbeing.

CHAPTER SIXTEEN

STRATEGIC INITIATIVES TOWARD A NEW ERA

He that is on a lee shore, and foresees a hurricane, stands out to sea and encounters a storm to avoid a shipwreck.[64]

Charles Caleb Colton

Our society is drenched in sex. We have been lulled into a stupor of collusion with the denigrating of sexuality by a deluge of cybersex and rampant sexualized industry. We are cut adrift from one another by our lifestyles. We are lonely. The epidemic of sex addiction is flourishing and we are *all* in the path of the storm.

Sex preoccupation is not a laughing matter anymore, nor is it a problem we can relegate to a marginalized subculture. As the storm of sex addiction widens, so should our concern about the problem and the factors that fuel it. We must resist the entropic status quo and find a new direction. But, where do we start?

In this chapter I will outline a few important initiatives that can help reverse the storm of sex addiction and launch a new paradigm for healthy sexuality. By responding strategically, we can unleash a tidal wave of positive social change, and begin a new era of respect for sexual dignity and sexual integrity as basic personal rights. These initiatives include the following:

- Exercise healthy sexual attitudes and choices in our personal lives

- Launch public education about the epidemic of sex addiction and the virulent addictive potential of cybersex

- Create public education about the illness of sex addiction and the possibility of recovery

- Educate the public about healthy and responsible sexuality, not just "safe sex"

- Provide quality education to youth about healthy relationships

- Support strong family life in which children can learn the basics of healthy relationships

- Encourage faith communities to provide education about the epidemic of sex addiction and about healthy and socially responsible sexuality

- Advocate local legislation requiring appropriate protections for children who access the Internet in schools and libraries or other public places

- Promote legislation requiring cyber-zoning of online porn sites similar to the land zoning of sex-oriented businesses, which protects both freedom of speech and the community welfare

Exercise Healthy Sexual Attitudes and Choices

Sex addiction thrives in a climate of devaluing and objectifying the sexuality of others. Practicing sexual respect in our personal lives, our social networks, and via our purchasing power is a potent antidote to the epidemic of sex addiction.

Despite the pornification of society, most of us agree that objectifying a person's sexuality and viewing it as a commodity is at a minimum disrespectful, and often exploitive. We share a general view that healthy intimate adult relationships are based on mutual consent and are free from compulsion, coercion, or exploitation. We believe that people should not be for sale and that it is wrong to take advantage of them on the basis of their gender or sexuality, especially children. The shocking scenes from Abu Gharib prison many years ago, hit a psychic nerve precisely because the sexual torture and humiliation of the prisoners violated our sense of basic human decency.

We can raise consciousness and affect change by acting on our better beliefs. The positive sexual attitudes that we model in our daily lives can be mirrored and amplified through our social networks and communities. For example, we can be powerful role models for youth and peers when we are mindful that our sexual comments do not degrade others, or we refuse to accept or pass along sexually demeaning images or jokes.

Likewise, the choices we make about the products we purchase (or refuse to purchase) and the entertainment we sponsor, make an impact on the marketplace and can ignite an influential chain reaction. Petitioning sponsors or boycotting products when they are sexually offensive and unhealthy is a powerful tool. People and products can be taken out of the market because of public outrage when they have stepped over the line. In addition, through the political process we can demand that our leaders model good behavior and respect the basic sexual rights of all persons.

Public Education about the Epidemic of Sex Addiction and the Virulent Addictive Potential of Cybersex

Sex addiction damages society and siphons valuable human and economic resources that support family and community life. It impacts all of us, directly or indirectly. Public education about the reality of the current epidemic and the dangers of cybersex, a leading contributor, are important in reversing the trend. Education could be conducted similarly to other successful campaigns, such as those against drunk driving, or the one for breast cancer awareness.

People need to understand the virulent addictive potential and other harmful effects of cybersex. For example, they should be warned that sex addiction can be self-induced by repeated exposure to Internet pornography, especially when the user is young, under high stress, or has previous history of trauma or addiction. The public needs to be made aware that cybersex can rewire a user's sexual arousal template and result in sexual dysfunction in his primary relationship; and that once this has occurred, the symptoms are difficult to treat. Parents need to know that children are vulnerable to cybersex addiction, and that it can have long term disabling effects on social development by crippling a child's ability to form intimate relationships. People need to know that behaviors that may at first seem innocuous—for example, frequently hooking-up or using iPorn—are uniquely risky and can be a gateway to the disorder.

Public Education about the Illness of Sex Addiction and the Hope of Recovery

Some people are embarrassed or disgusted by the subject of sex addiction, while others find it amusing. What talk show host or comedian did not draw a laugh with a joke about Tiger Woods or Charlie Sheen? Many people just consider sex addiction a lame excuse for questionable behavior. Because of these pervasive attitudes, the illness of sex addiction is often ignored, ridiculed, and misunderstood, much as alcoholism was years ago. Consequently, the sex addict and his family carry a heavy burden of shame and are reluctant to seek help.

Sex addiction is not about a "high sex drive," nor is it a harmless form of relaxation. It is not simply excessive sex, or sexual behavior one might find distasteful. It is a brain disorder characterized by cravings over which an addict has lost control, and compulsive sexual behavior that continues despite adverse consequences. People need an empathetic understanding of this devastating illness and the need for timely and effective treatment.

What can we do to promote public education about the illness of sex addiction and the hope offered by recovery? Word-of-mouth is the most powerful means of communication because each of us has credibility with those in our circle, and social media now multiplies the effect. We can make this book or numerous other resources on the subject available to our family, friends, clergy, and other helping professionals. We can invite knowledgeable speakers to groups with whom we are affiliated. We can initiate community education through our schools, churches, civic groups, public health departments, and child advocacy groups. We can encourage a friend or loved one who is in trouble with sexual behaviors to attend a 12-Step group or seek treatment. Efforts to create greater public awareness are not only good preventive medicine, but also make it more likely that sex addicts and family members can come out of hiding and get the help they need.

Healthy and Socially Responsible Sexuality

Guidelines for healthy sexuality might be compared to the lane markings on a highway. If we stay within them, we are more likely to get to where we want to go. If we do not, we may overturn in the ditch or collide with an oncoming car. So too with healthy sexuality, the choice to follow the guidelines is ours; but the tragedies that occur when we do not, are often shared by others.

Unfortunately, education about sexuality usually starts and stops with the basics of reproduction and "safe sex." Protecting from disease and preventing unwanted pregnancies is unquestionably important, but emotional and relational health is also at stake in intimate relationships. Comprehensive and effective education about healthy and responsible sexuality can be delivered through existing educational systems and personal networks.

Opinions on what constitutes healthy sexuality vary widely, but I believe most of us can agree that sexually healthy persons:

- Respect the wellbeing of themselves and partners and do not put self or others at physical, emotional, or spiritual risk (doing things against their beliefs)

- Respect the rights of others to self-direction and do not demand or threaten to extract sexual responses

- Do not use their authority over others (children, employees, patients, parishioners) to coerce sexual gratification, even if others are willing or seductive

- Respect sexuality as an intrinsic aspect of personhood, rather than treat it as a commodity, so they do not buy, sell, barter, or steal sex

- Do not *have* to act on sexual urges

- Respect vows of faithfulness and do not make excuses for infidelity in their primary relationship, or invite others to make excuses for infidelity

- Consider the consequences of their sexual behavior to self and others

- May have fleeting sexual thoughts and attractions but do not sexualize others with obsessive thought and fantasy without their permission

- Are honest with others about their intentions and do not deceive or manipulate the emotions of others for their own sexual pleasure or ego gratification

- Cultivate social interaction in the real world as the basis for building more intimate emotional and physical relationships, and do not have areas of their sexual lives that are secret or shameful

Public education about the real costs of anti-social sex, essentially behavior that ignores the above guidelines for healthy sexuality, is an integral part of reversing the epidemic of sex addiction. Reckless sexuality and overpowering others sexually is very destructive. It is irresponsible to minimize the impact of anti-social sexuality on victims or downplay the costs to society. Victims of sexual abuse often battle depression, suicidal thoughts, addictions, severe relational problems, and require mental health treatment. Through sexual betrayal, families are broken and partners are humiliated. Addiction related treatment and legal expenses may be sizeable and are sometimes paid by public funds. Whether symptomatic of sex addiction or the result of other issues, anti-social sexuality causes widespread damage and exacts a heavy toll.

Providing Quality Education for Youth about Healthy Relationships

Knowledge about healthy dating and sexuality is in the vital interests of our youth. It can help protect them from the dangers of cybersex and empower them against sexual exploitation and violence. It can guide them to more successful and satisfying relationships. It is our job as caregivers to protect and educate our vulnerable youth. We can protect them by providing information. They do not know that they can become addicted to porn. They do not know that if their arousal becomes associated with extreme images or experiences, their capacity to be attracted to real partners in the future may be impaired. They do not suspect that excessive online social networking may actually stunt their social development because it lacks so many of the dimensions of communication that are learned in face-to-face interactions. They seldom consider that contrary to the hype and the glamour of casual sex as promoted by the media and pop culture, it often results in personal and family tragedies.

Older children and adolescents need to be educated about the stages of intimacy and informed of the guidelines for healthy sexuality—the "rules of the road" for navigating the world of relationships wisely and safely. They need opportunities to candidly discuss these guidelines and their sexual questions and concerns with understanding adults. Young people should be taught that successful adult relationships are primarily based on emotional and social skills, not sex. They need to know that intimate experiences tap into the longings of the human heart, and if not handled with care, they can inflict painful feelings of rejection and loss when relationships are broken. They should be made aware that healthy intimacy is not just about performance and a fleeting experience of sexual pleasure, but about a deep consideration for another person.

Strengthening the Family as the Best Preventive Medicine

In healthy families and communities, children are nurtured and protected by caring adults who are emotionally present and interested in them. In strong families children naturally form positive core beliefs about themselves and learn to connect well socially. Chapters Fourteen and Fifteen are devoted entirely to the strengthening of family life because it is in that context that children acquire the best preventive medicine for sex addiction—the skills to form healthy relationships.

However, the family has never been able to go it alone, and certainly cannot do so in modern society in which mobility separates families from support systems, and negative social messages help unravel commitment bonds. As caring adults and communities, we can model commitment, teach and mentor, or offer a helping hand to young families or singles raising children. Relational awareness should extend beyond our own families; learn to create connectedness with others. A little support can provide essential strength or meaningful comfort for a family trying to hold things together.

Education Initiatives by Faith Communities

Faith communities are in a unique position to provide education about healthy sexuality, sex addiction, and the hope of treatment, by creating or expanding programs and ministries. Training of clergy and church leaders can prepare them to minister more effectively to individuals and families who are struggling with sex addiction, and to educate their members about the epidemic.

Churches should require pastors and staff to receive special training in sexual ethics, and volunteers should be educated about safe boundaries. There should be known procedures for reporting misconduct and protecting people when boundary violations are alleged or have occurred. Background checks should be conducted for anyone who works with youth, and there should be guidelines for the appropriate use of the Internet at church facilities.

Additionally, in healthy faith communities sexual curiosity is considered a normal part of the development of young people. Regard for sexual boundaries and freedom from coercion should be addressed as values of respect for self and others. Some churches have already designed age-appropriate curriculums for educating youth and parents about the normal experiences of sexual development, healthy dating, and sexual safety. Churches have a ready infrastructure that can be used for preventive efforts.

Legislation Requiring Cyber-Zoning of Online Porn Sites

The volume of pornography that is readily available and largely unregulated online is astonishing; but there are loud complaints if courts do not adhere to a broad interpretation of First Amendment free speech rights, under which pornography arguments are often made. However, the Supreme Court has determined that the government has the power to regulate sexually explicit material if it is considered obscene (lacking social importance and intended for sexual arousal); and for children, the government can prohibit access to sexually explicit material that it cannot prohibit for adults. But communities are left to decide what is obscene on a case-by-case basis.[65] And how can you really tell if someone accessing iPorn is an adult or a child? Having a clickable button that says, "I am at least 18," may not quite accomplish this objective.

As such, I propose that we launch a campaign for cyber-zoning that will require sexually explicit sites to use specific domain name extensions, perhaps ".xxx." That one seems appropriate. Cyber-zoning of online sex sites could parallel the model of the Supreme Court decision in *Renton v. Playtime Theatres, Inc.*.[66] This ruling allows communities to concentrate the zoning and placement of adult theaters or other adult-oriented businesses. They can be kept away from areas that may be harmed by "secondary effects." There is a substantial governmental interest in using zoning power to protect a community's quality of life. This zoning approach still allows for alternative avenues of "communication" for the sexually explicit material—freedom of speech—and does not get caught in the weeds arguing directly about "content."

Because of the unique nature of the Internet, it may be infeasible to implement online pornography zoning on a community-by-community basis; it may require a national approach. But I hope the *Storm of Sex Addition* has made the case that unlimited access to iPorn, in particular for children, produces harmful secondary effects on individuals, communities, and society. We would not expect parents to tolerate a steady stream of unsolicited shipments of unlimited quantities of alcohol and drugs to their homes for their children's sampling. We do not tolerate sex businesses on every block of the neighborhood and merely argue freedom of speech without any consideration for the community welfare. Nor should we expect families and communities to tolerate the dispensing of infinitely accessible pornography via the Internet. We can zone it.

Ending the Storm of Sex Addiction

By understanding the multiple factors contributing to the storm of sex addiction, we can develop strategic initiatives for effective responses at all levels of society. Education should be at the fore. In this chapter I have discussed nine possible initiatives—opportunities for each of us to be part of a national response team to reverse the public health epidemic of sex addiction. These are just the result of my brainstorming. Hopefully, you will have some good ideas you can contribute, too.

Our society has responded well to other public health and justice issues throughout our history. Public health education about early treatment and prevention of illnesses such as tuberculosis, smallpox, and polio virtually eliminated these diseases. Abolition, child labor laws, women's suffrage, and the civil rights movement are part of our struggle to live out the vision of freedom and protection from exploitation. Other addictions have been recognized and engaged with loving concern. When awareness of important issues reaches critical mass, it flashes like lightning into the consciousness of many. Citizens have seized the initiative and launched transforming movements and we can do so again. The renowned anthropologist Margaret Mead, after a lifetime of studying social dynamics, concluded, "Never underestimate that a small group of thoughtful, committed citizens can change the world. Indeed it is the only thing that ever has."[67]

Perhaps you are the citizen who makes careful choices to purchase goods that promote positive sexual messages and to avoid suppliers that use anti-social sexual advertising. Perhaps you are the parent who protects your family time and teaches your children respect toward self and others, including respect for sexuality. Perhaps you are the member of a policy organization that devises codes of ethics for the Internet industry, or develops protective policies for local libraries and schools. Perhaps you are the youth pastor who encourages a congregation to offer sex education and cyber-safety training for youth and parents. Perhaps you are the advocate for the cyber-zoning of Internet pornography. Perhaps you are the concerned professional, like me, who writes and speaks to educate others about sex addiction and treatment. Whatever your role may be, it is an important one to play.

If you understand the importance of the moment, please spread the word. There are already steady currents of positive change in response to the problem of sex preoccupation and sex addiction. The wave is growing and you can join this vital movement. Knowing the nature of the storm of sex addiction empowers us to be part of an effective response team to stop the epidemic and to begin a new era of respect for sexuality as an intrinsic aspect of personhood. We can learn to satisfy the deep longings of the human heart for love and connectedness— not with sex—but with genuine emotional intimacy in authentic relationships with ourselves and others.

ENDNOTES

1   Teilhard de Chardin, *The Divine Millieu* (New York: Harper Collins, 2001), 132.

2   The Society for the Advancement of Sexual Health (SASH) (statistics provided to SASH by David Delmonico).

3   Rip Corley and Deborah Corley (attributed to their presentation at the annual conference of the National Council on Sexual Addiction and Compulsivity in 1994, where they referred to online pornography as the 'crack cocaine of sex addiction').

4   Buzz Bissinger, "Tiger in the Rough," *Vanity Fair Magazine*, February, 2010.

5   Drew Pinsky, ET interview. CBS, December 4, 2009.

6   *See* Jeffrey Masson, ed., trans., *Complete Letters of Sigmund Freud to Wilhelm Fliess, 1887-1904* (Cambridge, MA: Harvard University Press, 1985), 287.

7   *See* American Psychiatric Association DSM-5 Development, "Proposed Revisions: Hypersexual Disorder," http://www.dsm5.org/proposedrevision/Pages/proposedrevision.aspx?rid=415

8   Susan Cheever, *Desire: Where Desire Meets Addiction* (New York: Simon and Schuster, 2008), 11.

9   *See* Helen Fisher, *Why We Love: The Nature and Chemistry of Romantic Love* (New York: Henry Holt and Company, 2004), 51-56.

10   Cheever, *Desire*, 17.

11   Leo Tolstoy, *A Calendar of Wisdom* (New York: Schribner, 1997), 49.

12   Gerald May, *Addiction and Grace: Love and Spiritually in the Healing of Addiction* (New York: Harper Collins, 1988), 14.

13   *See* Lauren Slater, "Love: The Chemical Reaction," *National Geographic*, February, 2006, 32-49.

14   *See* Patrick Carnes, *Facing the Shadow: Starting Sexual and Relationship Recovery* (Carefree, AZ: Gentle Path Press, 2010), 74-75 (Carnes discusses most of these elements as stages of courtship in adult relationships).

15   Carnes, *Facing the Shadow*, 76-78.

16   Marion Woodman, *Conscious Femininity: Interviews with Marion Woodman* (Toronto: Inner City Books, 1993), 45.

17   Patrick Carnes, *Don't Call It Love: Recovery From Sexual Addiction* (New York: Bantam Books, 1991), 109.

18   *See* Carnes, *Don't Call It Love*, 422.

19   *See* Isabella Hatkoff, Craig Hatkoff and Paula Kahumbu, *Owen and Mzee: The True Story of a Remarkable Friendship* (New York: Scholastic Press, 2006).

20   Zero to Three, "The 'Still Face' Experiment,'" http://www.zerotothree.org/child-development/early-childhood-mental-health/

21   Judith Herman, *Trauma and Recovery* (New York: Basic Books,1992), 1.

22   Harvey Jackins, *The Human Side of Human Beings: The Theory of Re-evaluation Counseling* (Seattle, WA: Rational Island Publishers, 1978), 46.

23   Carnes, *Facing the Shadow*, 5.

24   *See* Mardi Horowitz, *Stress Response Syndromes: Personality Styles and Interventions* (New York: Jason Aronson, 2002), 111-112.

25   Carnes, *Facing the Shadow*, 229-232; see also Patrick Carnes, Robert Murray, and Louis Charpentier, "Bargains With Chaos: Sex Addictions and Addiction Interaction Disorder," *Sexual Addiction and Compulsivity: The Journal of Treatment and Prevention*, 12:2-3 (2005), 98-113; see also Carnes, *Don't Call It Love*, 69-70; see also Harvey Milkman and Stanley Sunderwirth, *Craving for Ecstasy: The Consciousness and Chemistry of Escape*, (New York: Lexington Books, 1987).

26   Peter Trachtenberg, *The Casanova Complex: Compulsive Lovers and Their Women* (Crofton, MD: Poseidon Press, 1988), 28.

27   *See* Al Cooper, ed., *Cybersex: The Dark Side of the Force: A Special Edition of the Journal of Sexual Addiction and Compulsivity* (Philadelphia: Brunner-Routledge 2000), 2 (Cooper refers to an online "Triple-A Engine" of Access, Affordability, and Anonymity.).

28   *See* note 3.

29   Peter Steiner. Cartoon. *New Yorker*, July 5, 1993.

30   Patrick Carnes, David Delmonico and Elizabeth Griffin, *In the Shadows of the Net: Breaking Free of Compulsive Online Sexual Behavior* (Center City, MN: Hazelden, 2001), 22-25.

31   Albert Einstein, http://www.brainyquote.com/quotes/a/alberteins130982.html

32   *See* Carnes, *Out of the Shadows: Understanding Sexual Addiction* (Minneapolis, MN: CompCare Publishers 1992), 14-16.

33   *See* Patrick Carnes, *Contrary to Love: Helping the Sexual Addict*, (Center City, MN: Hazelden, 1989), 127.

34   *See* Carnes, *Out of the Shadows*, 9-12.

35   Old-timey carnival barker.

36   *See* Carnes et al., "Bargains With Chaos," 79-120.

37   *See* Carnes et al., "Bargains With Chaos," 87 ("[Addictions] in fact interact, reinforce, and become part of one another.").

38   *See* Patrick Carnes. Diagram. "The Black Hole – Addiction Interaction" (2004).

39   *See* Carnes et al., "Bargains With Chaos," 87-98.

40 Alice Miller, *The Drama of The Gifted Child: The Search for the True Self* (New York: Basic Books, 2008), 19.

41 Sexual Addiction Screening Test, http://www.SASH.net

42 M. Scott Peck, *The Road Less Traveled* (New York: Touchstone, 1998), 50.

43 Carnes, *Facing the Shadow*.

44 Charlotte Kasl, *Many Roads, One Journey: Moving Beyond the 12 Steps* (New York, NY: Harper Perrenial, 1992).

45 Robert Frost, "Revelation," *A Boy's Will* (New York: Henry Holt and Company, 1915).

46 Allan Schore, *Affect Dysregulation and Disorders of the Self* (New York: W.W. Norton and Company, 2003), flyleaf.

47 *See* Miller, *The Drama of The Gifted Child*.

48 *See* Alice Miller, *The Truth Will Set You Free: Overcoming Emotional Blindness and Finding Your True Self* (New York: Basic Books, 2001), x.

49 *See* Murray Bowen, *Family Therapy in Clinical Practice* (New York: Jason Aronson, 1982).

50 *See* John Bradshaw, *Homecoming: Reclaiming and Championing Your Inner Child* (New York: Bantam Books, 1990).

51 *See* Francine Shapiro, *Eye Movement Desensitization and Reprocessing: Basic Principles, Protocols and Procedures* (New York: Guiford Press, 2001).

52 Brenda Schaeffer, *Is It Love or Is It Addiction?* (Center City, MN: Halzelden, 2009), 13.

53 Romans 7:15 NIV

54 Focus on the Family. Poll. October 1, 2003.

55 *Today's Christian Women*, 25:5 (September/October, 2003), 58.

56 "The Leadership Survey on Pastors and Internet Pornography," *Christianity Today/ Leadership Journal*, Winter, 2001.

57 Mark Laaser and Louis Gregoire, "Pastors and Cybersex Addiction," *Sexual and Relationship Therapy*, 18:3 (August 2003), 397.

58 Ronald Richardson, *Creating a Healthier Church: Family Systems Theory, Leadership and Congregational Life* (Minneapolis, MN: Augsburg Fortress, 1996).

59 Mary Pipher, *The Shelter of Each Other: Rebuilding our Families* (New York: Balantine Books, 1996), 221.

60 Pipher, *The Shelter of Each Other*, 82.

61 Ron Kurtz, *Body Centered Psychotherapy: The Haikomi Method* (Mendocino, CA: LifeRhythm, 1990) (as quoted in Bradshaw, *Homecoming*, 288).

62 Daniel Goleman, *Emotional Intelligence: Why It Can Matter More Than IQ* (New York: Bantam Books, 1995), 43.

63   Mark Laaser, *Talking to Your Kids About Sex: How to Have a Lifetime of Age-Appropriate Conversations with Your Children About Healthy Sexuality* (Colorado Springs, CO: Waterbrook Press, 2004).

64   Tyron Edwards, ed., *A dictionary of thoughts: being a cyclopedia of laconic quotations from the best authors of the world both ancient and modern* (Detroit, MI: F.B. Dickerson Company, 1908), 102 (quoting Charles Caleb Colten).

65   *See* Ginsberg v. New York 390 U.S. 629 (1968); see also Miller v. California 413 U.S. 15 (1972).

66   *See* Renton v. Playtime Theatres, Inc. 475 U.S. 41 (1986); see also Young v. American Mini Theatres 427 U.S. 50 (1976).

67   Margaret Mead, http://www.interculturalstudies.org/faq.html#quote (According to the Institute for Intercultural Studies this quote "probably came into circulation through a newspaper report of something said spontaneously and informally. We know, however, that it was firmly rooted in her professional work and reflected a conviction that she expressed often, in different contexts and phrasings.").

RESOURCES

Sexual Treatment and Recovery Program (STARPRO)
www.connielofgreen.com

International Institute for Trauma and Addiction Professionals (IITAP)
www.iitap.com (*Certified Sex Addiction Therapists can be located by geographic area here*)

Society for the Advancement of Sexual Health (SASH)
www.sash.net

RECOVERY GROUPS

Sexaholics Anonymous (SA)
www.sa.org

Sexual Compulsives Anonymous (SCA)
www.sca-recovery.org

Sex Addicts Anonymous (SAA)
www.sexaa.org

Love Addicts Anonymous (LAA)
www.loveaddicts.org

Sex and Love Addicts Anonymous (SLAA)
www.slaafws.org

16-Steps for Discovery and Empowerment
www.charlottekasl.com

Celebrate Recovery
www.celebraterecovery.com

Co-Dependents Anonymous (CoDA)
www.coda.org

COSA
www.cosa-recovery.org

S-ANON
www.sanon.org

Recovering Couples Anonymous (RCA)
www.recovering-couples.org

Recommended Reading

Sex and Love Addiction

Out of the Shadows: Understanding Sex Addiction by Patrick Carnes

A Gentle Path Through the Twelve Steps by Patrick Carnes

Don't Call It Love: Recovery from Sexual Addiction by Patrick Carnes

In the Shadows of the Net: Breaking Free of Compulsive Online Sexual Behavior by Patrick Carnes, David Delmonico and Elizabeth Griffin

Facing the Shadow: Starting Sexual and Relationship Recovery by Patrick Carnes

Facing Love Addiction: Giving Yourself the Power to Change the Way You Love by Pia Mellody

Women, Sex and Addiction: A Search for Love and Power by Charlotte Kasl

Is It Love or Is It Addiction? by Brenda Schaeffer

The Porn Trap: The Essential Guide to Overcoming Problems Caused by Pornography by Wendy Maltz and Larry Maltz

Porn Nation: Conquering America's #1 Addiction by Michael Leahy

Desire: Where Sex Meets Addiction by Susan Cheever

Addiction and Grace: Love and Spirituality in the Healing of Addictions by Gerald May

Untangling the Web: Sex, Porn, and Fantasy in the Internet Age by Robert Weiss and Jennifer Schneider

Cruise Control: Understanding Sex Addiction in Gay Men by Robert Weiss

Ten Things Gay Men Can Do To Improve Their Lives by Joe Kort

Partners

Mending a Shattered Heart: A Guide for Partners of Sex Addicts ed. by Stefanie Carnes

Ready to Heal: Women Facing Love, Sex and Relationship Addiction by Kelly McDaniel

Deceived: Facing Sexual Betrayal, Lies and Secrets by Claudia Black

The Language of Letting Go by Melody Beattie

Codependent No More: How to Stop Controlling Others and Start Caring for Yourself by Melody Beattie

The Betrayal Bond: Breaking Free of Exploitive Relationships by Patrick Carnes

The Verbally Abusive Relationship: How to Recognize It and How to Respond by Patricia Evans

The Dance of Anger: A Woman's Guide to Changing the Patterns of Intimate Relationships by Harriet Lerner

PARENTING

Hyperstimulation: Teens, Pornography and Online Addictions by Craig Georgianna, Tom Underhill and Chad Kelland

Talking to Your Kids About Sex: How to Have a Lifetime of Age-Appropriate Conversations with Your Children About Healthy Sexuality by Mark Laaser

The Predator Next Door: Detect, Protect, and Recovery from Betrayal by Darlene Ellison

Parenting With Love and Logic by Foster Cline and Jim Fay

The Shelter of Each Other: Rebuilding Our Families by Mary Pipher

Reviving Ophelia: Saving the Selves of Adolescent Girls by Mary Pipher

Girl Wars: 12 Strategies That Will End Female Bullying by Cheryl Dellasega and Charisse Nixon

The Lolita Effect: The Media Sexualization of Young Girls and What We Can Do About It by M. Gigi Durham

Female Chauvinist Pigs: Women and the Rise of Raunch Culture by Ariel Levy

Emotional Intelligence: Why It Can Matter More Than IQ by Daniel Goleman

TRAUMA AND ATTACHMENT LOSS

Trauma and Recovery by Judith Herman

Treating Complex Traumatic Stress Disorders: An Evidence-Based Guide by Christine Courtois, Julian Ford, Bessel van der Kolk and Judith Herman

The Drama of the Gifted Child: The Search for the True Self by Alice Miller

Banished Knowledge: Facing Childhood Injuries by Alice Miller

Healing the Shame That Binds You by John Bradshaw

Homecoming: Reclaiming and Championing Your Inner Child by John Bradshaw

Silently Seduced: When Parents Make Their Children Partners by Kenneth Adams

Attachment in Psychotherapy by David Wallin

Affect Dysregulation and Disorders of the Self by Allan Schore

Affect Regulation and Repair of the Self by Allan Schore

The Developing Mind: How Relationships and the Brain Interact to Shape Who We Are by Daniel Siegel

Change Your Brain, Change Your Life: The Breakthrough Program for Conquering Anxiety, Depression, Obsessiveness, Anger and Impulsiveness by Daniel Amen

RELATIONSHIPS

The Couples Guide to Intimacy: How Sexual Reintegration Therapy Can Help Your Relationship Heal by Bill and Ginger Bercaw

How Can I Get Through To You? Closing the Intimacy Gap Between Men and Women by Terrence Real

Marriage Rules: A Manual for the Married and Coupled-Up by Harriet Lerner

Why We Love: The Nature and Chemistry of Romantic Love by Helen Fisher

Why Marriages Succeed or Fail and How You Can Make Yours Last by John Gottman

Erotic Intelligence: Hot, Healthy Sex While Recovering from Sex Addiction by Alexandra Katehakis

CLERGY

The Pornography Trap: Setting Pastors and Lay Persons Free from Sexual Addiction by Ralph Earle and Mark Laaser

Creating a Healthier Church: Family Systems Theory, Leadership and Congregational Life by Ron Richardson

Healthy Congregations: A Systems Approach by Peter Steinke

Sex in the Forbidden Zone: When Men in Power—Therapists, Doctors, Clergy, Teachers and Others—Betray Women's Trust by Peter Rutter

Acknowledgments

My heartfelt thanks to my son Ty, who suggested I write this book. He consulted with me in conceptualizing and organizing. He collaborated on writing and editing, and provided helpful original material. He generously invested his time and creativity throughout the process. His dedication inspired and motivated me and his sense of humor provided much needed levity and perspective during difficult phases of the work. I appreciate that he always believed in me, and did not say a single discouraging word throughout the effort. Thanks also to my son Blair, whose production and marketing expertise, and resources and coordination were invaluable in helping me get to the finish line and beyond.

My sincere thanks to Mary Pipher for reading the early manuscript and encouraging the project, and to Susan Lee Cohen, Riverside Literary Agency, for her guidance with writing and publication. Thanks to Jo Ann Miller for assistance with key sections in the proposal, and to Charlotte Sophia Kasl for her helpful suggestions. Thanks also to Kathleen Sullivan for her early consulting. My thanks to Marlys Oestreich and Jeanne Pettijohn for their excellent teaching and consultation in my CSAT training, and to Katherine Kent for her many years of guidance and wisdom. I would also like to thank Ralph Earle, Brenda Schaeffer, Kelly McDaniel, and Susan O'Day for their encouragement. Writers Susan Krause, Jeff Goudie and Tom Averill kindly listened to my ideas and shared their experience. I appreciate those who read chapters, including Rev. Evelyn Fisher, Holly, and Craig. My thanks to colleagues at Stonestreet Professional Services and Kairos Psychological, P.C. for their support and friendship, which helped sustain my energy. And thanks to my parents, daughter, Dan, and other family and friends who supported my efforts.

My sincere appreciation to Dr. Patrick Carnes for his visionary work, research, writing, and teaching, which has educated and guided so many clinicians like me and, in turn, brought the hope of recovery to countless suffering addicts and families. My thanks to many leaders in the fields of attachment theory, trauma, neuroscience, addiction, and psychotherapy, whose writing and ideas have contributed enormously to my work and life.

I also want to acknowledge the courageous men and women who shared with me the stories of their lives, and included me on their healing journeys.